BECOMING
L.O.V.E.

God's Guide to Choosing
LIGHT·OVER·VIBRATIONAL·ENERGY

C.H. Montgomery

ISBN: 978-1-7363995-0-7 (Paperback)
ISBN: 978-1-7363995-2-1 (Hardback)
ISBN: 978-1-7363995-1-4 (E-book)

Library of Congress Control Number: 2021900084

Any references to historical events, real people, or real places are sited as general references. Quotes from scripture are specifically taken from The Holy Bible, New International Version® NIV® Copyright© 1973, 1978, 1984, 2011 by Biblica, Inc.®

Published by CH Montgomery in the United States of America.

First printing edition 2021.

www.thekeystolove.org

These words are for seekers everywhere.

Contents

"In that day the deaf will hear the words
of the scroll, and out of the gloom and
darkness the eyes of the blind will see."
—Isaiah 29:18[1]

A Message from the Scribe

Those who seek God are promised that they will find Him. But for many, the journey is laden with traps and distractions. I am one of His servants who was invited to experience those traps.

Many years ago, I was told in a dream that I would be sent on a journey. At the time, I did not understand what this meant, nor could I have imagined the implications of this education or the power of the resulting instruction. Suffice it to say, everything I learned, I was guided to.[1] The Father sent me in, and the Father brought me out. He led me then, and He leads me now. His lessons for me were given in loving-kindness and for the sole purpose of relating information to those of you who have lived through similar things—specifically those of you who are seeking divine guidance.

---

[1] I want to make it perfectly clear that God did not send me into any situation to be deliberately misled or deceived. In an answer to prayer, He encouraged me to investigate a personal, energetic response to people and places that I have physically experienced since childhood. In the process, He allowed me to learn about supernatural gifts in settings outside of religion, and where seeking God first as the source of those gifts is not necessarily the prevailing view or the priority. This book came to me after these experiences, which served to help me understand the content, context and audience for whom it is written.

I acknowledge that "I" have had very little to do with this. Yes, I admit that I wrote down the words you will read in this text. And yes, I remember every day—every moment—of the process that was required to receive them. But these words are not mine—at least, not in the sense that they came from my own thoughts, my own opinions, my own knowledge. It would be much more accurate to say that I was simply an instrument that received them. That is what actually happened. Here's how it happened.

First, I am not a medium. I do not speak to "spirits" nor do I engage in any occult activity of any kind. What is contained in these pages is something entirely different. To "divine" an object typically involves the use of a device—for example, a person walking around with a divining "rod" that, when attuned to find a particular type of object such as metal in sand, emits a tone that allows the person holding the rod to locate the hidden item. Think of me as a rod that got attuned to a specific frequency that received information. This information has always been there. It has always been available to be received.

The most accurate way to explain the questions I am sure many of you will ask—why me? and why now?—is simply this: I was willing to be a receiver. I started a conversation with God (yes, the one and only creator of the universe talks to you if you ask Him to) and then I waited for Him to answer.

I did not move first.

I did not move at all.

I stayed still, and I listened.

That's it.

There's nothing special about me; anyone can receive Him. The hard part is getting rid of yourself—emptying who you are, what you think, what you fear, and what you believe in order to simply *receive*. Then, you have to learn to allow what comes to you to come without unintentionally interfering with it. Which, because we are all so full of ourselves, is not as easy as you might think.

So, let me explain what happened here. God sort of stalked me; He is actually stalking everyone—but in my case, He was especially persistent. At first, I did not want to do this and tried to deny that I could be a receiver of revelation. Yes, I said revelation. That is what lies within these pages. First, you should know that dreams, waking visions of angelic beings (which others saw and reported to me), preceded this process and I tried to ignore them all. Next, you should know that when I could no longer ignore what appeared to be a spiritual calling of sorts, I immediately (because I thought I was smart and knew a lot about religion) focused on all of the wrong things. So, I received a very thorough education on how to listen to what is "true" and how to discern what is deception. That education took almost seven years to unfold. During that time, not a word of this text was written. I did not begin to receive the "truth" until He decided that I was ready. I had nothing to do with the timing.

You may have noticed that I am putting the word "truth" in quotes. That is because it is important that you understand what His Truth actually means. Don't get hung up on the word that you think you know—I got stuck there for a while, too.

Throughout this text, God refers to "truth" in a very specific way. We know the word "truth" from its Greek origins, which is the word *Veritas*. In the Greek construct, truth is defined in a context that assumes a condition of duality. In duality, for one person to be right the other one must be wrong. In duality, there is good and bad, black and white, up and down; in this context, "truth" can only be obtained by finding facts (or evidence) that support one point of view and refute the other. That is NOT how God uses "truth".

God always refers to "truth" as the way that leads to a good result. Truth is God's process. And, He always means for us to use it in the context of His original words, conveyed in His original language of ancient Hebrew. In Hebrew, the word for "truth" is *Emeth* (pronounced eh'-meth). The closest translation we have of this concept is one that implies a person being able to know the path that bears good fruit—the sure way that leads to good things like peace, prosperity, abundance, ease, and joy. A path that leads to sorrow, turmoil, deception, pain, separation, chaos, or any other unfruitful thing is not the way that God intended life to be. And so, His Truth is about trial and error, tribulation and testing, and the surety of the way that arrives once you have experimented with false paths that only lead to folly. If you experiment with enough pain, you will eventually choose the way that leads to love, which is the most fruit-filled experience in the universe—if you can find it. And He wants to help you find it.

There are several words throughout this text that you will need to understand differently. For example, there are words in this manuscript that most of us have heard in a religious context that do not *only* mean what we thought they meant. These are words like love, faith, grace, peace, prayer, save, lost and many more. **It turns out these words have even deeper and more profound meanings; many of them are also acronyms that actually refer to entire concepts**. God refers to these as *"His words, behind His words."* Most of us know these words from religion. For those of you who accept God's words on faith, you do not need additional proof or even the additional insight provided in these deeper meanings. God knows you. You know Him. Nothing that He chooses to reveal here will change that.

We're all searching for answers that explain our place in the universe. So, although I am not going to take you on the personal journey of exploration that occurred before the inception of this book, I do want you to know that I have personally seen and experienced the attraction, fascination, and temptation to turn to spiritual tools as a means of confirming a divine connection. These tools seem to convey a power beyond what can be seen with the naked eye. There are "gifted" people who can see beyond our dimension. I am related to one of them. But what my journey and the resulting education were designed to teach me is this: **There is a difference between knowing that something exists and knowing the True path to everlasting life.** Seeing is not a form of believing that can be relied upon. In the end, only faith in God's ability to change us results in a true (sure) path to the higher dimensional existence we are all trying so desperately to find. Trying to gain access without God *always* ends in tragedy.

If you are someone who has tried every form of spirituality and found that your life is not fundamentally changed by your gifts, beliefs, meditations, or by the tools you rely on in your spiritual practice, then know this—this manuscript is for you. If the relating of this journey also speaks to Christians, then I am grateful to be of service to those of you who already accept God's guidance. This book was not written for you; however, God may use it to confirm what you have known all along. And if this confirmation strengthens you, then glory to God for using me in this way.

For those of you who have been seeking "good" without seeking God, He wants to clear up a few misconceptions. Many of His words have been twisted, redefined, manipulated, and used out of context. That does not change the power of them for those who know Him intimately and personally. But for the rest of humanity, those looking for love in all the wrong places, talking to the wrong "gods" and "guides," He says it's time to talk about these words in a different way. In this text, He provides you with the opportunity to understand and to discern His Truth without further interference or manipulation and to reveal aspects of His nature directly and personally to you by way of relationship and epiphany. He also provides a scientific context for His words as well as a broader spiritual meaning (beyond traditional religious doctrine) for those who require "evidence" or have had a negative experience with religion. He knows that there are many who cannot accept the aggressive use of His words when they are used as an excuse by warring factions around the world claiming to be acting on His behalf or fighting for His glory or any other such misuse of His intention.

In this text, He also speaks from three different perspectives. Do not be confused when it sounds as though He is speaking one moment and then you read something that sounds like "I" am speaking to you. Except for what I have contributed in the introductions to each section of this book, I am not the author. I am just the **S.C.R.I.B.E.: Sanctified and Consecrated Receiver of Information Begat in Eternity.** He often speaks as the triune entity that He is— Father, Son, and Holy Spirit. When He speaks as the Father, you will easily understand His words from that point of view (we're all used to thinking of Him that way, and I have tried to draw your attention to His words from that point of view by noting that The Father is speaking and italicizing them). When He speaks as Son, sometimes it is from His experience as a human being who walked the Earth, and sometimes it is from His perspective as the unique spirit designed for communion with God the Father (for this reason the Son's words will also be set off in italics). When you see a phrase containing "we" it is often meant two ways—the personal relationship or experience shared between the two of you, and the collective relationship or experience humanity has as part of the one body and mind of God.

The advice imparted here is His Truth (the way that leads to a good result) given to me throughout my own journey. In my journey, I have also been directed down many false paths for the purpose of understanding the fruitless things mankind uses in our efforts to transform ourselves and, in that process, bolster the belief that by simply "being good" people, obtaining "knowledge," and relying on discipline alone, we can overcome our natural tendencies and, in general, improve our condition in the world.

What has been made abundantly clear is this: without God's grace to accompany our every move, we take missteps that repeatedly lead us into experiences filled with deception and pain. Since I am what most people would consider a "good" person who doesn't stray very far from society's rules or beliefs about what it means to "be good", the false paths I have experienced are minor compared to the pain and suffering many others have experienced, and yet, they are still deadly.

I thank God that in my years of intense and personal instruction I never lost sight of God's presence and His power. Even when terribly confused and lost in chaos, I always returned to His will and gave up my own. He led me into places and to people deliberately enamored with their own power for a reason—to show me the futility of their struggle and the fragility of their faith. I saw things that are hard to understand, let alone believe. And the worst part is that initially, they were extremely attractive because they appeared to be designed *to help people*. And to some extent, they even appeared to work. But in the end, every single person, tool, and healing ritual ceased working, and the lack of any true (sure, steadfast, faithful) *real* power in them became a personal, first-hand source of knowledge for this book.

So, this is for seekers everywhere. This first volume is one of three manuscripts that have already been received and written down. The second and third will be revealed when He instructs me to release them. "Becoming L.O.V.E." is His introduction to what is actually happening, and always has been. This book is for those of you looking for the sure way to experience unending, undying, unwavering, unconditional love. I guess that includes just about everyone.

PART 1

Becoming L.O.V.E.

Love

What is Love? It is all that matters. It is a state of being, an act that is not just an emotion. The closest thing mankind has to the true experience of "love" is what you call a feeling of "joy" combined with a feeling of "peace." But to truly be in **L.O.V.E.** means to exist in a state of being that is unwavering and unchangeable.

L.O.V.E.: Light Over Vibrational Energy

Like God Himself, this state of being is at one with all that exists. You often call it unity with God or bliss—an experience of "perfection." However, being at one with all is more than bliss. When acting from L.O.V.E., it is possible to eliminate all strife, suffering, pain, and loss. Even death disappears because none of those things exists in the state of L.O.V.E.

Is it possible to become L.O.V.E. itself? Yes. But there is only one process that gives human beings access to L.O.V.E. at the highest realm. And to achieve L.O.V.E. as a state of being, one must choose to be changed by God Himself. With transformation, a new state of being arises from *a new being*—one that is divinely created and *adapted for unity with Him.*

How is this possible? Through an energetic connection that allows for transformation to take place—a bridge that transfers our soul's pleas for release from the prison of the mortal body. What is the source of this connection? It is God Himself.

It is important that as you read these words, you allow yourself the freedom to believe in the possibility that love is more than you understand it to be and that L.O.V.E. is capable of reaching out to you personally. May each seeker that comes this way find the One designed to deliver you to the divine destiny that has eluded you for so long.

CHAPTER 1

Life

The Father Speaks...

*There is an energy that binds all life together in an interwoven fabric of information and light. It is unlike any energy in matter and contains only pure potential for good. Within this "fabric" of life there have been two distinct and opposing networks, or paths—unity and duality. One promotes cooperation and co-creation seamlessly with the source of all. One network brings My will for all, from the source of all, using L.O.V.E. This **O.N.E.** network is **Omnipresent Neutral Energy**, and it protects and preserves (pre-serves) all living things. I call it **L.I.F.E.** for it is the very fabric of the creation—the conduit for light through which all things receive My will for them.*

O.N.E.: Omnipresent Neutral Energy

L.I.F.E.: Light Inside the Fabric of Eternity

The other network destroys L.I.F.E. It is a counterforce, originating from a source inside anti-matter's density and darkness. The "other" is emitting a vibrational sequence of wavelengths at the sub-atomic level, designed to interfere with the creation—to prevent all things from receiving *unfettered L.O.V.E. from the Source of all. You do not realize that this other network exists, and the closest thing you imagine it to be is something you have named "dark matter." I named it **S.A.T.A.N.** because it is the Sub-Atomic Transmission Altering Neutrality.*

S.A.T.A.N.: Sub-Atomic Transmission Altering Neutrality

*Together, in unity, these two forces once worked to allow a harmonious transfer of information and potentiality to manifest in matter, specifically to human beings from the Source of all L.I.F.E., from the giver of L.O.V.E. But now, these two forces are at war. O.N.E. pre-serves your heart and mind for the purpose of reigniting and reestablishing the seamless connection from Source to soul to manifestation in matter by way of L.O.V.E. **O.T.H.E.R.** seeks to destroy all L.I.F.E. by way of fear.*

O.T.H.E.R.: Omnipresent Transmissions Heating/Hating Emmanuel's[1] Resonance

O.T.H.E.R.'s intention is to rule the creation from its own source—a source born in darkness. You may ask, why was this dark source ever created if it's very presence threatens all of L.I.F.E.? That is difficult to explain. However, the easiest way to understand it is to consider that the

---

[1] Emmanuel means "God with us". Spelled with an "E" the name refers to His eternal presence, and when spelled with an "I" refers to God made flesh, or God near us. (http://www.preceptaustin.org/immanuel-emmanuel.htm, updated 12-18-17)

original design did not contain the source of darkness within the body of L.O.V.E. nor did I intend for the option of free will (experimentation outside of the direct influence of L.O.V.E.) to be corrupted to the extent that you would never know Me.

*You have heard that "to know Me is to love Me"? This is Truth. For in very practical terms, I Am the Way, the Truth and the Life in you. To **K.N.O.W.** Me is your choice and has always been so.*

K.N.O.W.: Know No O.T.H.E.R. Way/Wavelength

---

*But to choose to traverse L.I.F.E. without L.O.V.E.'s direction and protection should not result in **D.E.A.T.H.**.*

D.E.A.T.H.: Dissonant[2] Energy Altered Through Heat/Hate

---

*I Am revealing this information and its relationship to your condition at this time for several reasons—most importantly, that this is the time foretold (spoken into being) long ago before the **W.O.R.L.D.** began. But also,*

---

[2] There are many definitions and examples of resonance versus dissonance because both terms are applied to a variety of lines of study including chemistry, physics, music, psychology and so on. This use of the word dissonance as part of the acronym for "death" is intended to refer to anything that opposes resonant energy, unity, accord versus discord and so on. The basic definition of dissonance, as defined by Merriam-Webster simply means "a lack of agreement" Dissonance." Merriam-Webster.com Dictionary, Merriam-Webster, www.merriam-webster.com/dictionary/dissonance. Accessed 22 Oct. 2020.

because you are at the critical juncture—the crossing that exists for those choosing L.O.V.E. over all O.T.H.E.R. paths.

W.O.R.L.D.: War of Rebellion in L.O.V.E.'s Domain

Soon, those who have been woven into the fabric of L.I.F.E. and adopted into the family of L.O.V.E. shall be collected for manifest eternity's final chapter—the ultimate re-creation of all in L.O.V.E. divine (of the vine). Those who have come to K.N.O.W. Me by way of surrender to L.O.V.E. are being transformed. They are being changed from within the body to embody energies solely designed to support L.I.F.E. And in the end, they will be separated from all O.T.H.E.R.

*The choice to come to L.O.V.E. is yours. But I will not allow the blind to be left behind to **D.I.E.** without understanding the choice that they are making.*

D.I.E.: Disintegrate Internally and Eternally

S.I.N. *is a deception that blinds you to the "nature" of all things and, in the process, corrupts you.*

S.I.N.: Satan's Interfering Network

You seek "love" and to be "good," and yet, you do not understand that the opportunity before you is not about "being good." It is about being transformed into something that is literally good—an extension of God, a being that is completely integrated into the nature of God. Neither you nor your world is capable of becoming L.O.V.E. on your own because you are imprisoned by something that you cannot see and yet believe is normal. You "think" that what you currently experience is just the way things really are, and that your adherence to society's rules and religious doctrine is the way to "be good."

You understand that you are part of something larger than yourself; therefore, on some level you understand that you are not a completely independent, self-governing entity. But the more important thing to note is that because you are a part of the O.N.E.-ness of all things, the very idea of self-reliance is used to imprison you. Instead of Becoming L.O.V.E., you strive to love O.N.E. and O.T.H.E.R. through your own effort and through adherence to ideas about "love" that are fundamentally incomplete.

I do not say this to condemn or threaten. No, I tell you this so that you might see the way offered through the energetic lens of creation, and not through the intellectual or emotional state of mind that is continually plagued by S.I.N. The truth is that your emotions do not serve the highest **G.O.O.D.**

G.O.O.D.: God's Omnipresent, Omnipotent Domain

They serve your mind's attempts to manage experiences in the physical world. But it is a false experience that is rooted in Satan's Interfering Network. Your emotions are not essentially good or bad—as the enemy would have you believe. They are simply energetic and chemical responses to stimuli transferred by a neural network that is embattled in duality. Your mind is fragile as a result of continual bombardment by the wavelengths of S.I.N. Therefore, it cannot serve the highest G.O.O.D. until it is free to become L.O.V.E., to be remade as part of the O.N.E. And so, it is written that those who come to the Father by way of His **S.O.N.** *shall find peace.*

S.O.N.: Spirit Offered in Neutrality

But without the L.O.V.E. of the O.N.E. sent to **S.A.V.E.**, *guiding you through the maze of deception, your chances of finding L.O.V.E.'s home are nonexistent.*

S.A.V.E.: Sanctify[3] Against Vibrational Energies

It is not because I do not wish to see you again. I L.O.V.E. you beyond measure. But I cannot allow you into the realms of heaven as you are. I cannot see you again until you seek Me and are fully robed in **G.L.O.R.Y.** *And the evil that binds you to your present condition continually erodes you, even unto death, without L.I.F.E. to sustain your days.*

G.L.O.R.Y.: God's L.O.V.E. Omnipresent and Resonating in You

---

[3] To Sanctify is to make holy. (Definition of "sanctify" from the Cambridge Academic Content Dictionary, copyright Cambridge University Press)

*Do not think that I am unable to bring you—for nothing is stronger than the bond created in L.O.V.E. by L.O.V.E. itself, and those who choose My network shall rise to meet Me. Be among them. Unplug from the network of S.I.N. and reboot your very soul on the path to becoming L.O.V.E. Come to Me and **R.I.S.E.***

R.I.S.E.: Reside/Re-side Inside the Sanctity[4] of Eternity

---

[4] "The generic meaning of sanctification is "the state of proper functioning". To sanctify someone or something is to set that person or thing apart for the use intended by its designer. A pen is sanctified when used to write. Eyeglasses are sanctified when used to improve sight. In the theological sense, things are sanctified when they are used for the purpose God intends." (From Baker's Evangelical Dictionary of Biblical Theology-Sanctification. Copyright 1996. Taken from biblestudytools.com) In the context given here, sanctity is also meant to emphasize a state of being that, once made holy, is inviolable.

Chapter 1: Life

O.N.E. Omnipresent, Neutral, Eternal
L.I.F.E. Light Inside the Fabric of Eternity
L.O.V.E. Light Over Vibrational Energy
S.A.T.A.N. Sub-Atomic Transmission Altering Neutrality
O.T.H.E.R. Omnipresent Transmissions Heating/Hating
   Emmanuel's Resonance
K.N.O.W. Know No O.T.H.E.R. Way/Wavelength
D.E.A.T.H. Dissonant Energy Altered Through
   Heat/Hate
W.O.R.L.D. War Of Rebellion in L.O.V.E.'s Domain
D.I.E. Disintegrate Internally and Eternally
S.I.N. Satan's Interfering Network
G.O.O.D. God's Omnipresent, Omnipotent Domain
S.O.N. Spirit Offered in Neutrality
S.A.V.E. Sanctify Against Vibrational Energies
G.L.O.R.Y. God's L.O.V.E. Omnipresent and Resonating
   in You
R.I.S.E. Reside/Re-side Inside the Sanctity of Eternity

CHAPTER 2

Time

The Father Speaks...

*When I created the world, I gave it the innate power to self-govern. Time is the construct for the experience of the creation. Time was created to aid the development of diversity and variety of life through the intermingling of species. Experimentation was part of the plan from the beginning. Those who think it was an "accident" are missing the bigger picture. A static world without change would not support the needs of the plants and animals I placed here. Only a vibrant, evolving world with adaptability built into its "nature" provides the sort of experience I/We are seeking. Creation is ongoing, and in the world, humans were designed to be co-creators. Together, with Me, we were meant to design and manage the creation. This is the reason that you were envied and despised by those who seek to destroy you. They wanted the ability to create. They thought they deserved to be here, experiencing the act of creation for themselves. And they mistakenly assumed that the experience of co-creating would involve only their own desires, and not Mine. They wanted their own **K.I.N.G.D.O.M.**

K.I.N.G.D.O.M.: Kinetic Integration into Neutral G.O.O.D./God's Design of Omnipotent Manifestation

*In a dance of co-creation, time is fundamental. It is the means by which we plan each manifestation of L.I.F.E. Time serves to guide the development of L.I.F.E. at various stages. Without a "time-clock," growth does not take place. In fact, growth is not possible. Manifestation of perfected life forms only comes through their growth and development into maturity. **T.I.M.E.** is essentially the means for growth.*

T.I.M.E.: Temporal Insights Meted in Eternity

*I made mankind differently. I perfected him in the original design. As a co-creator, perfection insured that our management of the world would take place in "paradise"—in a state and through a process that only yielded joyful and fruitful manifestations. T.I.M.E. was always there before the fall of man, but T.I.M.E. was not slowed down beyond that which was necessary for growth. In the original design, manifestations occurred quickly because T.I.M.E. moved faster than what you experience today. Once the **F.A.L.L.** occurred, the vibrational level both of mankind and of the world (because you are linked to the creation of the world metaphysically) slowed down to the lowest, densest, and slowest timetable.*

F.A.L.L.: Forbidden Access
to L.O.V.E.'s Light

*This was a precautionary step required to ensure that negative thoughts, manifestations, and creations could not materialize so rapidly that any one "thing" could overtake the world. Slowing time kept **E.V.I.L.** manifestations from conquering all of creation. Slowing T.I.M.E. significantly protected the rest of creation from the manifestations of the W.O.R.L.D. by further separating it.*

E.V.I.L.: Energetic Vibrations
Inverting L.I.F.E.

Christ says...
*As the breach in your mind and body is healed, time returns to the speed and to the level of being originally intended. I Am drawing closer. You are drawing closer. Together, we are managing the healing process in accordance with The Father's **W.I.L.L.** and not in submission to the brokenness of man's mind.*

W.I.L.L.: Word and Intention in L.I.F.E.
and L.O.V.E.

This is why the only way to experience the paradise originally intended for man's existence is a change in the vibrational resonance of the Earth. Earthquakes, volcanoes, and other natural phenomenon are responding to the increasing speed and changes in time-space density. As I come closer to you, and you to Me, we change the vibrational level of all experience. We will "merge" in a dance of co-creation that allows for all "life" to benefit. Disease, suffering, blight, drought, pain, and other conditions that plague the planet now will not be present in the new world because the new vibrational state of the world will not support the vibrational states created during the period of time that has been marked as "the fall of man." When you R.I.S.E., all of life rises with you.

Chapter 2: Time

K.I.N.G.D.O.M.: Kinetic Integration into Neutral
  G.O.O.D./God's Design of Omnipotent Manifestation
G.O.O.D. God's Omnipresent, Omnipotent Domain
L.I.F.E.: Light Inside the Fabric of Eternity
T.I.M.E.: Temporal Insights Meted in Eternity
F.A.L.L.: Forbidden Access to L.O.V.E.'s Light
L.O.V.E.: Light Over Vibrational Energy
E.V.I.L.: Energetic Vibrations Inverting L.I.F.E.
W.O.R.L.D.: War Of Rebellion in L.O.V.E.'s Domain
W.I.L.L.: Word and Intention in L.I.F.E. and L.O.V.E
R.I.S.E.: Reside/Re-side Inside the Sanctity of Eternity

CHAPTER 3

Jesus

L.O.V.E. took the form of a man for one reason: to remove the chains that bind us to the wrong network. Our lives are not our own. They are given to us as a part of the divine experience of L.I.F.E. as a whole. We are connected to the stars and to the bodies that govern the cosmos. And our manifestations are likewise connected to the larger environment in which we operate—the world. That is why it was necessary for us to be separated from the cosmos. Until we choose to be part of the grand plan, and not in competition with it, our "home" remains elusive. Our experiences bring us in contact with God's design or they bring us in contact with evil. Evil is L.I.F.E. threatening. **E.V.I.L. is the antithesis of God's design, and it has its own special vibrational sequence that, when activated, creates opposition to life-giving processes.**

For example, when you see a child in the arms of its mother and you witness what we call "unconditional love" at work, the mother and the child thrive. They grow together and, in many ways, develop abilities that each could not experience on their own without the presence of the other and "love." The reverse is also true. When a crime is committed, and people are victimized, they feel damaged because they *are* damaged. Their trust and faith in a system designed to protect them has failed. This is essentially the state we find ourselves in—a state of being that fails to protect us from destruction. D.E.A.T.H. is the by-product of our current attachment to the network of **F.E.A.R.**

F.E.A.R.: Foreign Energy Altering Reality

Our separation from L.O.V.E. has placed us in a pickle. What to do, when nothing you can accomplish on your own will change the conditions in which you live (and die)? You cannot make the vibrational sequence set in motion resonate at a different level unless you have the ability to resonate at another level as well. Remember, we are connected to creation and it to us and (unfortunately) to the wrong network. The consequence of this unholy trinity is pain and D.E.A.T.H. But, if you take one piece of that puzzle and purify it until its resonance is aligned with L.O.V.E., how might you change the entire sequence? How might the vibrational levels of all involved be affected? That is Christ's mission—to change willing hearts and to purify them. It's that simple. Once changed, you become a person who is resonating L.O.V.E., and in turn, your world is positively affected by your personal **H.E.A.R.T.** resonance.

H.E.A.R.T.: Heaven's Eternal Alliance Resonating Truth

As we change into L.O.V.E. our world changes with us. Natural shifts in the form of hurricanes, volcanoes, and earthquakes are not isolated incidences of nature. They are responses to the changing vibrational levels of all that is within our ability to co-create. God has told us that He is with us always. He means that His presence is in everything and throughout everything in creation. He also means that He stands beside us unconditionally—always and in all ways. His L.O.V.E. is the most powerful force in the universe; so, it should not be difficult to understand that when we are told to ask in the name of **J.E.S.U.S.**, we are being given the key to unlocking power beyond our own abilities.

J.E.S.U.S.: Jehovah's Eternal Spirit Under[1]/Unified in the S.O.N.

When we cooperate with God, we generate His light and His L.O.V.E. and we are simultaneously tapping into the network originally designed to bring us the experience of peace, joy, and love. So why do we continually struggle to maintain peace, even after we have accepted the gift of J.E.S.U.S.' presence?

Because we fight the darkness of the competing network daily. The ability to overcome and destroy the compromised connections to our present condition happens slowly. Like a weaver sewing a blanket, we are being reconnected to the proper channels and disconnected from the damaging ones. Our power source cannot be turned off completely without also turning off our life force, but its course can be altered piece by piece. So, change is slow to come even when we are praying for it. The process of becoming L.O.V.E. is slowly changing each of us from the inside out. But, when we forget what God has taught us and reconnect to the network of

---

[1] Being "under" the S.O.N. denotes the authority given by the Father to the S.O.N. to perform this work for the whole of creation. The unity of all is also obtained through the S.O.N.—Spirit Offered in Neutrality.

darkness, we are inadvertently reconnecting to damaged circuitry and are in danger of falling backward into a state of being that can harm us, again and again. This is why Jesus called us to live in **P.E.A.C.E.**

P.E.A.C.E.: Predominating Energy with Acceptance of Christ Eternally

---

When Jesus said the greatest commandment is to "love God with all of your heart and mind and spirit and strength, and love one another as you love yourself,"[2] He wasn't just talking about being "nice" to each other. He was referring to an *act* of love. He was telling us that our hearts, minds, spirits, and strength would be capable of complete and un-fettered love if we committed our entire selves to God; and that through this active process of becoming L.O.V.E. we would be brought into a permanent state of peace and joy. **He was telling us that we are able to change because He is able to change us.**

But only if we accept His way—because there is only one way provided by God Himself. There is just one "name" strong enough to "save". And that **N.A.M.E.** is J.E.S.U.S.— who also happens to be the Way, the Truth, and the L.I.F.E.

N.A.M.E.: Neutral Amalgam in Manifest Eternity

---

[2] The Holy Spirit is making a reference to scripture here from the Holy Bible-Matthew 22: 37-39, specifically when Jesus answered the Sadducees question, "Which is the greatest commandment?"

Chapter 3: Jesus

L.O.V.E.: Light Over Vibrational Energy

L.I.F.E.: Light Inside the Fabric of Eternity

E.V.I.L.: Energetic Vibrations Inverting L.I.F.E.

D.E.A.T.H.: Dissonant Energy Altered Through Heat/Hate

F.E.A.R.: Foreign Energy Altering Reality

H.E.A.R.T.: Heaven's Eternal Alliance Resonating Truth

J.E.S.U.S.: Jehovah's Eternal Spirit Under/Unified in the S.O.N.

S.O.N.: Spirit Offered in Neutrality

P.E.A.C.E.: Predominating Energy with Acceptance of Christ Eternally

N.A.M.E.: Neutral Amalgam in Manifest Eternity

CHAPTER 4

The Way

Christ Says...
The way forward is elusive for those outside of My pro-
tection. A rocky road would best describe the experience
they are having. In time, they will be unable to withstand
the ups and downs. When I Am present in the life of a per-
son (a child of God), I Am orchestrating even the smallest
things in that person's day. A smile at a moment when it's
needed most. A stranger passing by that reminds them to
be thankful, giving them a sense of well-being despite hard-
ship. Those are the little things. But I Am capable of large
and bold movement in a life when I Am asked to step in and
take over.

Why do you need Me to be present in your mind and
heart? A person's heart cannot generate the level of light
needed to draw God's best to them unless that heart has
been healed. I Am the healer. When you are being tested,
your heart is also tested. Strong hearts withstand dire cir-
cumstances by knowing that all is well. At another level of
existence, the changed heart knows that the power behind
all of creation is at work in everything because the changed
heart intuits the power of My presence in them and in the
world. A hardened heart hears nothing, sees nothing, and,
in effect, misses the evidence of My hand at work in their
life. As time goes on, their ability to recognize those with

changed hearts is also limited. They see only hardship because hardship is what they experience.

It is important to remember that hearts are changed when children give themselves to the Father through Jesus Christ. The way is narrow, because the Father's L.O.V.E. can only be delivered by His Deliverer. When Christ. is the anchor in your life, and you trust that His way is the way to receive God's best gifts, especially the gifts of peace and grace, then all is well because the way has been prepared in advance, and the outcome is assured. The bridge is intact. The passage is clear. The **W.A.Y.** *is not littered with stumbling blocks.*

W.A.Y.: Wavelength Abiding in Yahweh[1]/You

His path is easy compared to the path laid out by the evildoers of the world. When you engage with those who are planning deceit you agree to walk a path that is not meant for those with changed hearts. You will find that your heart can't "take it" anymore. Your natural ability to abide (work alongside) with the people of the world is weakened, while your ability to rise above the chaos created by them is strengthened. I Am is behind this process.

The final result is a separation of heart and mind for those following My path from the hearts and minds of those following the world's path. Ultimately, the separation in-cludes physical displacement as well. When the time comes,

---

[1] Yahweh (pronounced Yah-Way) is the Hebrew word for the holiest name of God, meaning "I Am". It is also the word used to name God by many American Indian tribes. The first use of this name in the Bible occurs in Exodus 3: 13-15 and it is the name by which God chooses to be known in the context of His relationship with people throughout all generations.

I will bring My people out of harm's way by removing them from the dangers awaiting those who are committed to the way of the world. I will remake the world and, in the process, eliminate the path of the wicked. Those outside of My protection when this process begins will be sacrificed unless they call upon the Lord's name (J.E.S.U.S.) for salvation. Those who do will be rescued from death but will have to endure the changes taking place in the world until the new world is ready for My return and rule. At that time, all will be judged according to his deeds. Because, unless he has turned his life over to Me to be changed, his only defense is righteousness—has he walked a path that has been good, despite his belief in the world? Or has the world shaken the foundations of his character in ways that have led to D.E.A.T.H.?

The W.A.Y. is narrow, but it is easy compared to the path of the world. Everyone who walks with Me walks in grace. Everyone who knows My voice knows peace. All else becomes unimportant in their hearts and minds. When you see someone desperately clinging to their life, tell them to let go of it and gain everlasting peace and life by taking the path that leads to everlasting redemption. Let Me come into your heart and take it over. Let Me come into your life and remove the pain and the struggle before the end of T.I.M.E. Allow Me to lead you to safety in the days remaining, and I will deliver you to the O.N.E. for the rest of time.

ACRONYM GUIDE

Chapter 4: The Way

L.O.V.E.: Light Over Vibrational Energy
W.A.Y.: Wavelength Abiding in Yahweh/You
J.E.S.U.S.: Jehovah's Eternal Spirit Under/Unified in the S.O.N.
S.O.N.: Spirit Offered in Neutrality
D.E.A.T.H.: Dissonant Energy Altered Through Heat/Hate
T.I.M.E.: Temporal Insights Meted in Eternity
O.N.E.: Omnipresent, Neutral, Eternal

CHAPTER 5

Christ

The W.A.Y. forward is a narrow passage, through a single **H.U.M.A.N.** being that transcended the world and resides nearest to the Source of all.

H.U.M.A.N.: His Ultimate Manifestation Abiding in Neutrality

Through **C.H.R.I.S.T.** we are able to reconnect with God's original intention for mankind.

C.H.R.I.S.T.: Consecrated, Holy, Resonating & Indwelling Spirit of Truth

---

Intention is a key element in the entire process of creation. When God thinks of something positive and beautiful, it manifests in L.I.F.E. God is pure L.O.V.E.—goodness in all thought and deed. However, when the vehicle of manifestation is separated from the intention to produce that which is only G.O.O.D., the potential to produce "shadows" of the original thought is enhanced. As you move further away from God's presence, the intention is further compromised by competing thoughts. **Mankind essentially fell from proximity to God and His intentionality.**

We made a choice to anchor our reality in a faraway place. We did not know when we made this choice that the consequences of our actions would result in separation that left us vulnerable to thoughts and actions that are counter to joy and peace. But the introduction of E.V.I.L. thought—the simple awareness of it—placed us in a continual condition of "indecision."

Before we were separated from God's presence, we knew His mind—meaning that we understood His intention and naturally, telepathically translated His thought into our own being. We were at O.N.E.—body, spirit, and mind—in the sense that, as co-creators, our abilities to manifest only "good" thoughts and G.O.O.D. things were protected by our close connection—our proximity to God/G.O.O.D. Mankind was originally placed second in the hierarchy of all creation, above even the angels. Why would God do this? Because His intention was to manifest His **B.E.I.N.G.** in a physical state for the purpose of experiencing His most physical form of creation.

B.E.I.N.G.: Benevolent Entity Interred in Neutral G.O.O.D.

Angels are spirit. God is spirit. Man is physical. The Father needed a God-Man in His creation to experience all that He created and loved into being. His desire was for a partner that would transcend the temptation to create anything except L.O.V.E. Notice I said "desire" and not command *or* intention? He desired a partner but gave us free will to reject that partnership if we chose to do so.

You may recall the biblical story of angels who rebelled against God? Some of the spirit-angels created at that time were jealous of God's abilities and domination over all things. Some of them tried to change the order of creation and actually attacked the Father in His own domain—creating a state of B.E.I.N.G. that (prior to this action) did not exist. **Rebellion created a vibrational frequency of great suffering—something that was the exact opposite of God's nature/God's vibration/God's intention.** All of creation was affected by the introduction of this vibration. **W.A.R.** was created in the form of competing intentions (competing vibrational frequencies).

W.A.R.: Wavelengths Attacking Resonance

Suddenly, the natural order of thought was inverted, and two potentialities existed. So, God banished those spirits who rebelled and sentenced them to a state of being that requisitioned and confined them to the lowest vibrational form of existence: the physical realm.

When we read about the "serpent" in the garden, it is not a literal serpent, but rather a reference to the lowest vibration (wavelength)—something so low that within the physical realm it would be inert, unable to even walk upright. Slithering on its "belly" is simply a description designed to give us a sense of how low these beings were in the order of existence. For these beings, "fallen" meant banished to the lowest realm, the farthest place away from the presence of God Himself, with no possibility of return. This was done for the protection of all creation.

Unfortunately, the lowest vibrational existence was in Earth's dimension—the physical realm. No other form could imprison and hold the rebels in a way that separated them from the spirit realm. Only the physical realm provided a significant barrier to the spirit realm. So, God sent them here and bound them in the Earth, as a **V.I.R.U.S.**

V.I.R.U.S.: Vibrations Inert of Resonance Under Spirit

Talk about low—to go from angelic states of being to something so inert that they could not take on any other form of being, except for one possibility: if a co-creator with the innate power of God could be used to transform them into something else.

Now will you understand the series of events? It was not God's intention but it was always God's plan. Before T.I.M.E. existed, before the Earth was formed, He knew what the outcome of the creation must be. The W.O.R.L.D. was created to correct counter-vibration, and **H.U.M.A.N.I.T.Y.** was and is the answer to the restoration of peace.

H.U.M.A.N.I.T.Y.: His Ultimate Manifestations Abiding in Neutrality's Infinite Truth as Yahweh/You

---

It doesn't seem possible, does it? That God would know before creating the Earth, and mankind, and everything in it, that this could happen. But He did. He suggested that man be made in His own image for a reason—to create a W.O.R.L.D. and a being that would ultimately remake *everything* in His image, even the angels. Our ability to correct the order of creation was dependent upon once knowing God so intimately that we would crave His presence for all eternity. So, He originally made us *like* Him and placed in us a thirst for Him that could never be quenched, until all that was created is realigned with His original state of B.E.I.N.G. **A part of God Himself was compromised, and only a part of Himself could undo His own counter-vibrational creation.** Enter mankind and the W.O.R.L.D. to fall and to be banished, but also ... to be redeemed.

C.H.R.I.S.T., the perfect God-Man, is His means of redemption. When God sent His **O.N.L.Y. S.O.N.**, He was sending a part of Himself to suffer the H.U.M.A.N. experience and live in the counter-vibrational form of existence *to overcome it through the indwelling power of His own presence in this state of being.*

O.N.L.Y. S.O.N.: Omnipresent Neutral Light of Yahweh's Spirit Offered in Neutrality

---

He came to this level of the creation to restore it, using His original intention and the power that only He has—the power to change the world from what it is to what it should be. Now, will you **S.E.E.**?

S.E.E.: Seek, Experience, Enlighten

The Consecrated, Holy, Resonating, Indwelling Spirit of Truth is the *only* W.A.Y. because God's presence had to be re-seeded here, and Christ was the first unblemished God-Man to inhabit the world since the F.A.L.L. By overcoming D.E.A.T.H.—which only God could do—and making disciples with a commission to do the same, He created a way forward—the W.A.Y.

It is not an accident that man's path has been rocky. Trial and error are part of the way forward, like the ebb and flow of tides. Why? Because only a perfect God-Man could navigate the world without continually falling or making mistakes that compromised His state of being. Our ability to navigate the world is very weak without God's indwelling spirit of **Emeth**[1]. The Jewish people were given "rules" to live by as a means of coping with the counter-vibrational tendencies that lead to death and destruction until the cure could be introduced into the world.

C.H.R.I.S.T. is the cure.

The Healer came to "die" so that in this realm of existence His spirit could both abide with us and be close to God at the same time *and beyond time*. He transmits both God's power and His intention to us when we invite Him in to do so. When we attempt "healing" on our own, we find that eventually the world brings us back to places of darkness, sadness, temptation, and turmoil. Why? Because we are compromised beings that carry within us the seeds of both G.O.O.D. and E.V.I.L.—we are no longer exactly like Him. At best, we are dim reflections. But we are given the possibility of being a God-Man, of becoming L.O.V.E., of being

---

[1] Emeth (also Emmet, Emet) is the Hebrew word for truth. You will find many definitions and debates about the underlying meaning of this word and its biblical implications and applications; however, almost all scholars acknowledge that the root word for all other definitions of truth are based in the ancient Hebrew concept of truth, not the Greek word Veritas. The Hebrew word for truth contains the first letter of the Hebrew alphabet, the middle letter and the last, implying that truth endures from beginning to end and refers to something that both endures and never ends. For the purposes of this text, God wishes for you to think of it as the sure and steadfast path to a good result—the way that emerges in relationship with Him.

like Christ. We cannot overcome the W.O.R.L.D. without Him, and His S.O.N. *is* Him in human form. **So, remembering is more than reconnecting to a memory of who we once were, it's "re-membering" by reconnecting with God Himself.** And in the process, it's allowing Him to redesign our ability as co-creators (with O.N.E. heart and mind) for *only* G.O.O.D. thoughts and *only* G.O.O.D. intentions. This is why only those with *like minds* will be permitted to return **H.O.M.E.**

H.O.M.E.: Holy O.N.E.s Manifesting in Emeth/Eternity

Those who remain undecided remain divided, and nothing divided will stand. As Earth is renewed, only those who have undergone the process of becoming L.O.V.E., becoming O.N.E. with God, will be able to remain in and with Him. Humanity's task is to make up individual minds for C.H.R.I.S.T. — O.N.E. at a T.I.M.E. and then to allow Him to heal our hearts and unify our collective mind (collective conscience) in accord with His mind: God's/G.O.O.D.'s vibration. He has promised that all who choose to remain apart from the O.N.E. will perish in the "**L.A.K.E. of F.I.R.E.**"[2]

---

[2] The "Lake of Fire" is described in the Bible in the book of Revelation, Chapter 20, verses 10 and 14-15.

L.A.K.E. of F.I.R.E.: Life's Alternate Kinetic Experience of Foreign, Inverted Rebellious Energies

Christ says...

"Those who know Me hear My voice. I Am able to guide them to places of safety because they listen for My instruction. Those who receive instruction from any other voice are being misled, for none of the spirits of the natural world, the underworld, or the afterlife have knowledge of the Father. I am in Him and He is in Me. If you remain in Me and I in you, you will bear much fruit. Apart from Me you can do nothing, but through Me all things are possible."[3]

This is "Truth" at its very essence. Truth is not a belief system that separates right from wrong. **Truth is Emeth: the sure and steadfast way of L.I.F.E.** Life is either flourishing or dying, at all times. The way that leads to abundant life is joyful and peaceful and is through J.E.S.U.S. C.H.R.I.S.T. and His connection to the Father's power to give L.I.F.E. The way to D.E.A.T.H. is any way that is not grounded in C.H.R.I.S.T., which is in turn grounded in the Father (Source). Those who persist in worshipping or relying on their own power, or the advice of spirit guides who claim to have ascended to the "highest" realm of knowledge, are committing the same original mistake that started the process of man being separated from God.

Deception is the very nature of "original sin" (separation) and the belief that doing anything without God's involvement is possible. The entities who tell spiritualists

---

[3] Christ's comment here is nearly identical to what Jesus said to his disciples in the book of John, Chapter 15: 4-5.

and channels that they can help them achieve nirvana and that they "know the way" are being untruthful, because *there is no other W.A.Y.* than through C.H.R.I.S.T. the **L.O.R.D.**

L.O.R.D.: L.O.V.E. Overtaking Rebellious Domains

The God-Man of all creation made a way through Himself for His creation to be renewed. No "other" way produces the cure. No "other" way provides the permanent healing that comes from the Father of all things. Relying on a rock, a totem, or an intermediary who claims connection with the spirit world is the equivalent of reliance on false gods. False gods have no power to redeem the creation. At best, O.T.H.E.R.s have mastered the art of energetic interference—which is counter-productive to the power that God offers to heal you. It may feel like it helps you temporarily—but ultimately the power of any object fades away. **The only life force you can rely on fully and completely to bring you into the state of being that resides with God is God Himself.** Compatibility with any "other" thing in creation *traps your being* in a state that is lower than the state reserved for God-Men, and outside of the proximity of God's presence.

Those who choose to remain outside of God's presence are on a path that leads to self-destruction. The W.O.R.L.D. is on that path, but those in God's light, those in His presence, those in His L.O.V.E., are being renewed and restored to His original state of **G.R.A.C.E.**

G.R.A.C.E.: God's Resonating Alliance in C.H.R.I.S.T. Eternal

Do not be caught outside of the state of G.R.A.C.E.—for once the window has been closed and the tribulation begins, those outside of God's protection will endure great suffering before a final blow is dealt. The W.A.Y. is easy for those who choose the narrow gate. There is no way for all O.T.H.E.R.s.

Chapter 5: Christ

W.A.Y.: Wavelength Abiding in Yahweh/You
H.U.M.A.N.: His Ultimate Manifestation Abiding in Neutrality
C.H.R.I.S.T.: Consecrated, Holy, Resonating and Indwelling Spirit of Truth
L.I.F.E.: Light Inside the Fabric of Eternity
L.O.V.E.: Light Over Vibrational Energy
G.O.O.D.: God's Omnipresent, Omnipotent Domain
E.V.I.L.: Energetic Vibrations Inverting L.I.F.E.
O.N.E.: Omnipresent, Neutral, Eternal
B.E.I.N.G.: Benevolent Entity Interred in Neutral G.O.O.D.
W.A.R.: Wavelengths Attacking Resonance
V.I.R.U.S.: Vibrations Inert of Resonance Under Spirit
T.I.M.E.: Temporal Insights Meted in Eternity
W.O.R.L.D.: War Of Rebellion in L.O.V.E.'s Domain
H.U.M.A.N.I.T.Y.: His Ultimate Manifestations Abiding in Neutrality's Infinite Truth as Yahweh/You
O.N.L.Y. S.O.N.: Omnipresent Neutral Light of Yahweh's Spirit Offered in Neutrality
S.E.E.: Seek, Experience, Enlighten
F.A.L.L.: Forbidden Access to L.O.V.E.'s Light
D.E.A.T.H.: Dissonant Energy Altered Through Heat/Hate
S.O.N.: Spirit Offered in Neutrality

H.O.M.E.: Holy O.N.E.s Manifesting in Emeth/Eternity

L.A.K.E. of F.I.R.E.: Life's Alternate Kinetic Experience of Foreign, Inverted Rebellious Energies

J.E.S.U.S.: Jehovah's Eternal Spirit Under/Unified in the S.O.N.

D.E.A.T.H.: Dissonant Energy Altered Through Heat/Hate

L.O.R.D.: L.O.V.E. Overtaking Rebellious Domains

O.T.H.E.R.: Omnipresent Transmissions Heating/Hating Emmanuel's Resonance

G.R.A.C.E.: God's Resonating Alliance in C.H.R.I.S.T Eternal

Entering The Kingdom

The way is narrow, but it is open to all. When you accept the gift of God's presence in your heart and mind, you are essentially surrendering the belief that you are able to find your way on your own. Those who come to the Father through C.H.R.I.S.T. need not worry about knowing how it all works or even if it is working on a metaphysical level. They only need to let go of their own power source and replace it with Mine.

We have discussed the networks and the choice that must be made—choosing the path of life that is offered through the spirit of C.H.R.I.S.T. guarantees connection to My **T.R.E.E. of L.I.F.E.**, My network of influence.

**T.R.E.E. of L.I.F.E.: Truth Resonating
in Eternity's Energy of Light Inside
the Fabric of Eternity**

C.H.R.I.S.T. is your anchor and will never fail to bring you through the darkness if you are surrendering to My guidance and not striving or struggling to become L.O.V.E. on your own.

The way is easy when you surrender your own will, because the underlying current is that of divine design. It automatically takes you along the path to righteousness (right living). Like floating in a stream to a river and on to the ocean, and then experiencing the wonders of the deepest parts of yourself, you find a new way of living through **F.A.I.T.H.** and G.R.A.C.E.

F.A.I.T.H.: Forever Accepting the Interred Truth in Him

However, if you struggle and paddle and attempt to navigate using tools or means of your own making, you will inevitably find your effort bringing you back to old patterns of behavior and ways of thinking.

Why? Because your life experience dominates your understanding without My presence to override your life-to-date programming. You go with what you think you know. I go where the Father leads. Your ability to override your human nature is compromised by a divided mind, and your physical separation ensures a path that loops back upon its own knowledge. It is not meant to be a trick. It's just part of the design. This design was a necessity once man chose the path of knowledge, or **D.E.M.O.N.S.**

D.E.M.O.N.S: Destructive Energies/Entities Manifesting in Omnipresent Neutral Spirit

---

The Father made a way to protect the rest of creation from interacting with what is essentially a self-destructive cycle, destined to test its limits and, in the process, damage those attaching to the wrong network.

Christ says...

I Am able to bring H.U.M.A.N.I.T.Y. out of the cycle because My life gave the Father the means to reinstate His network. Like a seed planted in the W.O.R.L.D. to grow and to die and to transcend, beyond the limits of human experience, My Spirit is offered as a bridge to a new path, one that does not loop inward on itself but rather carries pilgrims seeking the Father directly to Him. I Am "seated" at the right hand of God in the sense that We are connected energetically as O.N.E. mind. I Am the only "Son" (offspring) in the sense that only My spirit K.N.O.W.s His mind. I Am able because He made me in this W.A.Y. and for this purpose. I alone am given the divine blueprint of His intention—the means to understand all that is planned for the redemption of mankind and the nature of the change needed to ensure your return to E.D.E.N.

E.D.E.N.: Eternity's Dominion of Energetic Neutrality

I Am the deliverer—the means to make the changes that will carry you H.O.M.E. to the G.L.O.R.Y.[1] of His presence and the end of suffering.

G.L.O.R.Y.-2: G.O.D.'s Light and Omnipotent Residence in You

---

[1] This is a second acronym for GLORY and refers to how we will experience His glory once all is accomplished in C.H.R.I.S.T. When we are "at home in glory" all will be O.N.E. in the light of His presence (and prescience). In our present state GLORY is part of the process of God's Love Overcoming Rebellion in You.

But, the time for coming across the bridge is ending. The time for becoming L.O.V.E. is being sped up for those who say, "Yes, I will come." One day soon, you will S.E.E. Me. And, on that day, all will know that I Am able, that I Am the W.A.Y. But for those who are not already crossing over, the W.A.Y. will disappear and only darkness will remain. When the light leaves, those trapped in darkness will find only F.E.A.R. and suffering. Do not be one of them. Do not allow darkness the means to keep you trapped in its web of deceit. Give your life to the light. Give your struggle to the Father. Let Me take your petition to Him who waits to cover you in G.R.A.C.E.

Chapter 6: Entering The Kingdom

C.H.R.I.S.T.: Consecrated, Holy, Resonating and Indwelling Spirit of Truth

T.R.E.E. of L.I.F.E.: Truth Resonating in Eternity's Energy of Light Inside the Fabric of Eternity

L.O.V.E.: Light Over Vibrational Energy

F.A.I.T.H.: Forever Accepting the Interred Truth in Him

G.R.A.C.E.: God's Resonating Alliance in C.H.R.I.S.T Eternal

D.E.M.O.N.S.: Destructive Energies/Entities Manifesting in Omnipresent Neutral Spirit

H.U.M.A.N.I.T.Y.: His Ultimate Manifestations Abiding in Neutrality's Infinite Truth as Yahweh/You

W.O.R.L.D.: War Of Rebellion in L.O.V.E.'s Domain

O.N.E.: Omnipresent, Neutral, Eternal

K.N.O.W.: Know No O.T.H.E.R. Way/Wavelength

O.T.H.E.R.: Omnipresent Transmissions Heating/Hating Emmanuel's Resonance

W.A.Y.: Wavelength Abiding in Yahweh/You

E.D.E.N.: Eternity's Dominion of Energetic Neutrality

H.O.M.E.: Holy O.N.E.s Manifesting in Emeth/Eternity

G.L.O.R.Y.-2: God's Light and Omnipotent Residence in You

S.E.E.: Seek, Experience, Enlighten

F.E.A.R.: Foreign Energy Altering Reality

CHAPTER 7

Fear

There is only one way to overcome F.E.A.R. Fix your eyes on J.E.S.U.S. Be still and know that He is able to overcome any and all F.E.A.R. He did it in His life on Earth, and He is even more able in His present state to do it in yours. When you surrender to God's G.R.A.C.E. and acknowledge that He alone is able to counter the effects of F.E.A.R., you will experience what is known as "the peace that passes under-standing."[1] Your mind and heart are flooded with a sense of peace and security. All seems well, because in spite of your circumstances, the Truth (Emeth) is all *is* well. **Fear is not a state of being, but rather a wave of deception that is sent from your mind to your heart.**

When you believe the lies that promote thoughts of F.E.A.R., your heart and ultimately your body are riddled with the wavelength that manifests as "fear." This is easy to overcome, because it is confined to your personal state of being and not manifest in the world, unless and until you speak it aloud and promote the thoughts that created it in you, in others. **God is not trying to scare you. People are.**

---

[1] The "peace that passes understanding" is referred to often as a state of being that is different than the type of peace of mind that is hard won, tenuous and fragile. The apostle Paul refers to this type of peace in his letter to the church at Philippi, in the book of Philippians 4: 7

When you fix your eyes on God, you can see that His presence is more powerful and not subject to the "fears" of men. He transcends F.E.A.R. When you are abiding with Him and Him with you, together you rise above the tendency to succumb to F.E.A.R. "Fear" is powerful because of its ability to paralyze you and to create hopelessness. But "fear" is nothing compared to the power of "hate." What good men create can easily be destroyed when mankind chooses to "hate."

Hatred is the most destructive, negative wavelength. It is the strongest E.V.I.L. wavelength being manifested through mankind. Hatred not only invades life it also undoes it. Other negative emotions do personal, internal damage, but the wavelength of hatred erodes your life at its source, your life's force. Hatred does not damage the person it is directed to as much as it damages *you.*

Let's be clear here—it is important to understand that God does not *manifest* "fear" or "hatred." We do. As co-creators, we are endowed with the ability to manifest either good or evil, depending upon our thoughts, feelings, and actions. But God has never, and will never, *manifest* E.V.I.L. things. Our choices determine what we experience, and those choices determine what others experience. When more people turn to God and surrender to His W.I.L.L. (over their own), there is a natural inclination toward good. God is *only* L.O.V.E. God is *only* peace. God's presence in your heart and mind produces more love in your life. By "love", I do not mean romance, nor do I mean better people around you. I mean *you.*

He changes what you feel and think, and He even changes what you are made of because you have voluntarily given Him permission to do so. Your acceptance of His W.I.L.L. delivers His grace. G.R.A.C.E. unfolds as you learn to recognize His hand in your life's way. His instruction retrains your heart and mind, but His power (and light) also remake you into a being that is not subject to F.E.A.R., but rather, someone who is **A.B.L.E.** (like Christ) to overcome it.

A.B.L.E.: Abiding in the Benevolent Light of Eternity

The manipulations and lies of people who have not chosen L.O.V.E., who have not allowed J.E.S.U.S. into their lives, continue to be made manifest through an unrepentant will. Their state of being is a chaotic state of mind. Until and unless they surrender to the only power that can change that for them, they will gravitate toward thoughts and behaviors that support their belief in their own power. Again, let's be clear. "Hate" is the most powerful human emotion, and unlike "fear" that targets and initially affects your individual state of being, "hate" compels people to act against another. "Hate" manifests in the world as actions that cause pain in another person. But **H.A.T.E.** is futile, because it is a lie.

H.A.T.E.: Hell's Alienating Thought Energy

In reality, all is well. In the end, all will be revealed, and those choosing H.A.T.E. over L.O.V.E. will be removed from the rest of creation. God will not allow those choosing H.A.T.E. to enter into His unified state of G.R.A.C.E.—His K.I.N.G.D.O.M. of L.O.V.E. and light. H.A.T.E. has no place there, because the only vibration that exists with God and His people is the all-powerful, all-consuming state of B.E.I.N.G. known as L.O.V.E. It's what He (and eventually you) are made of.

Chapter 7: Fear

F.E.A.R.: Foreign Energy Altering Reality
J.E.S.U.S.: Jehovah's Eternal Spirit Under/Unified in the S.O.N.
S.O.N. Spirit Offered in Neutrality
G.R.A.C.E.: God's Resonating Alliance in C.H.R.I.S.T Eternal
C.H.R.I.S.T.: Consecrated, Holy, Resonating and Indwelling Spirit of Truth
E.V.I.L.: Energetic Vibrations Inverting L.I.F.E.
L.I.F.E.: Light Inside the Fabric of Eternity
L.O.V.E.: Light Over Vibrational Energy
W.I.L.L.: Word and Intention in L.I.F.E. and L.O.V.E
A.B.L.E.: Abiding in the Benevolent Light of Eternity
H.A.T.E.: Hell's Alienating Thought Energy
K.I.N.G.D.O.M.: Kinetic Integration into Neutral G.O.O.D./God's Design of Omnipotent Manifestation
G.O.O.D.: God's Omnipresent, Omnipotent Domain
B.E.I.N.G.: Benevolent Entity Interred in Neutral G.O.O.D.

CHAPTER 8

Grace

Christ says...

The word grace comes from the Hebrew meaning for two camps—decision and indecision. Those who are decidedly "all in" for God/G.O.O.D. are often begat the ability to S.E.E. with correction at each step. Although they L.O.V.E. Me, they still rarely look forward to being corrected without fear of shame. This takes many experiences with Me to overcome, but eventually, all F.E.A.R. is given over to the way of L.O.V.E. Those who are but halfway "in" are not aware of the effect of any indecision and, in these moments, are continually being corrected without the foreknowledge of the misstep. G.R.A.C.E. begins, both before (indecision) and after (decision). G.R.A.C.E. never ends, even until the final day. All shall be clothed in righteousness, but also covered in G.R.A.C.E. No perfect H.U.M.A.N. exists today in the world—all are corrupted by S.I.N. But soon no imperfections shall remain in those who move into "Holy Matrimony"[1]— a state of union with the divine that is unchangeable by F.E.A.R. And yet, while still in the W.O.R.L.D., they shall be assaulted by S.I.N. and subject to correction.

---

[1] Throughout the Bible there are references to a day of reunion with God that are described in terms relating to marriage. The church is repeatedly referred to as the Bride of Christ.

*Both camps receive My G.R.A.C.E. when they call upon My N.A.M.E. It is a different response, depending upon where the traveler is on his or her journey. But G.R.A.C.E. is available to both. To the O.N.E. and the O.T.H.E.R. My G.R.A.C.E. is the same. It matters not which "stage" you are in—the response when you call upon Me by N.A.M.E. is the same, for mine is the N.A.M.E. above all names. The real question is, will you call upon Me for the benefit of your brother without seeing the plank in your own eye? Will you run to the altar in thanksgiving for your own salvation without pleading for the wayward brother's life? Will you turn toward the light, accepting all that you have been told and taught for the true experience of My H.E.A.R.T., or will you burn for the "truth" you think you know through reason and doctrine and understanding? Or, will you be the "heart" of My H.E.A.R.T.—the O.N.E. who L.O.V.E.s beyond dissention, beyond reproach, beyond failure, beyond fruitlessness? If you can see that the way of Truth bears good fruit (and I Am the W.A.Y.), why can you not see that the way of G.R.A.C.E. is equally fruitful? Why can you not acknowledge that My sovereignty in all matters makes that which is born into matter more fruitful when you allow Me to bestow all involved with G.R.A.C.E.? Why do some say, "I am here, Lord," and yet fail to see that their brother is not absent from My K.I.N.G.D.O.M. as they would assume him to be? Both are camped inside the walls of L.O.V.E. divine. Both have taken their own paths to find the fruitful ground for L.I.F.E. to blossom. Both have tainted their ground with false praise and folly. But neither are **L.O.S.T.** from G.R.A.C.E. (to corruption). All that is needed is L.O.V.E.'s redeeming G.R.A.C.E. (for correction).*

L.O.S.T.: Living Outside of the Spirit of Truth

*Ask for My **H.A.N.D.** in forgiveness of all, and both the sinner and the saint in O.N.E. shall be given G.R.A.C.E.*

H.A.N.D.: Heaven's Alliance in Neutral Dominion

For this is the way of the Lord Jesus Christ—to forgive, even when they know not what they do. But as you become L.O.V.E., the way to understanding is opened. Let the eyes S.E.E. Let the H.E.A.R.T. follow. Let the mind release the pattern and path established thus far on the journey. And let all be covered by G.R.A.C.E.

Chapter 8: Grace

G.O.O.D.: God's Omnipresent, Omnipotent Domain
S.E.E.: Seek, Experience, Enlighten
L.O.V.E.: Light Over Vibrational Energy
F.E.A.R.: Foreign Energy Altering Reality
G.R.A.C.E.: God's Resonating Alliance in C.H.R.I.S.T Eternal
C.H.R.I.S.T.: Consecrated, Holy, Resonating and Indwelling Spirit of Truth
H.U.M.A.N.: His Ultimate Manifestation Abiding in Neutrality
S.I.N.: Satan's Interfering Network
W.O.R.L.D.: War Of Rebellion in L.O.V.E.'s Domain
N.A.M.E.: Neutral Amalgam in Manifest Eternity
O.N.E.: Omnipresent, Neutral, Eternal
O.T.H.E.R.: Omnipresent Transmissions Heating/Hating Emmanuel's Resonance
H.E.A.R.T.: Heaven's Eternal Alliance Resonating Truth
W.A.Y.: Wavelength Abiding in Yahweh/You
K.I.N.G.D.O.M.: Kinetic Integration into Neutral G.O.O.D./God's Design of Omnipotent Manifestation
L.I.F.E.: Light Inside the Fabric of Eternity
L.O.S.T.: Living Outside of the Spirit of Truth
H.A.N.D.: Heaven's Alliance in Neutral Dominion

CHAPTER 9

Peace

Mankind seeks "peace"—in his life, in his work, in his mind. But peace is tentative at best when it is dependent upon those around you to be maintained. This is why the kind of peace man seeks is impossible without the transformation of all. Imagine a world where all people are able to overcome fears that lead to unrest—all of the time. Sound like a dream? It's not; it's a design that is supported by the Creator of all things, preferred by the universe, and held in tact for those who are not separated from God/G.O.O.D.

When you come to the Father through His S.O.N., you are walking the path that allows you to receive the gift of P.E.A.C.E. And God gives everlasting peace. It is a state of being in and of itself—independent of other states of being— and able to consume all other wavelengths (derivatives[1]) because His very essence is L.O.V.E. *Agape* is what the ancients called it, and it is all consuming. You have heard of the first commandment—"Love the Lord your God with all

---

[1] Here God is referring to energetic alterations of His original thought/wavelengths. We typically define a derivative as "something having qualities taken from something else. If something is derivative, it is not the result of new ideas, but has been developed from or copies something else." Definition of derivative from the Cambridge Academic Content Dictionary© Cambridge University Press.

your heart, mind, spirit, and strength."[2] **This is *not* a request to dedicate your emotional life to God.**

It is an invitation to be *transformed* by Him into a B.E.I.N.G. that is A.B.L.E. to overcome all other emotional states in favor of the state of L.O.V.E. He can and will consume everything else that competes with L.O.V.E. if you ask Him to. Understand that His state of being has nothing to do with "romance." It does not rely on another being to be ignited or "felt" in your heart. It never dims with time, never becomes stale or boring. The "love" you know relies on interactions with other human beings to be felt, and it also relies on them to be maintained. God's L.O.V.E. is a state of being that most closely resembles what we might experience as peace combined with joy—a frequency that is both ecstatic and calm at the same time. It is a way of interacting with yourself and the world that is protected by God Himself, because it *is* God Himself, living in you. When you allow the S.O.N. to deliver God's P.E.A.C.E. in your heart and mind, you are accessing a way of being that is protected by the Father at all times. Once you have been transformed through His power, there is nothing that can reverse the transformation except your own rejection of it, and even then, you must consciously and willfully deny Him as your **S.A.V.I.O.R.**

S.A.V.I.O.R.: Spirit Abiding Vibrational Incarnation to Overcome Rebellion

---

[2] There are ten commandments listed in the Bible, originally given to Moses to share with the Hebrews during their time wandering in the desert. This is a reference to the first commandment spoken into being at that time, which Christ repeats centuries later in Matthew 22:37 when asked; what is the most important commandment?

No O.T.H.E.R. person can steal your P.E.A.C.E. No O.T.H.E.R. situation can rob you of the understanding that *all is well*. But let's be completely clear about one thing. **Peace cannot be attained through your own effort. It is a gift from God, one that requires communion with God to access.** No man possesses this kind of P.E.A.C.E. in himself naturally, and none can offer it to you. It is easy to see in those who know God intimately, personally, and wholly, because you can see their transformation. But to know it in that way for yourself, you must first take the W.A.Y. that leads to peace. J.E.S.U.S. is *the* W.A.Y. He alone is in a position to access God's essence and transmit it to you. Energetically, C.H.R.I.S.T. is the only B.E.I.N.G. anointed (appointed) for *this purpose*. There is only O.N.E. W.A.Y., and He's it.

I want to take a moment to emphasize that this is not about believing in a specific religion—it's about accepting the S.O.N. of God, the only aspect of Himself that is offered to you in a permanent and perfected state of energetic neutrality.

So, when someone says to you, "Just trust in J.E.S.U.S.," what they are trying to convey, even without understanding the scientific basis and underlying physics behind that statement, is that trusting in the S.O.N. to bring the Father's L.O.V.E. into your heart and mind is the way to find "peace" and that it occurs through an energetic transformation. You will find permanent P.E.A.C.E. and not just temporary relief. They say, "The W.A.Y. is easy and the burden is light,"[3] and now, perhaps you can understand that with God working His transformative power in you, it really is.

---

[3] The Holy Spirit is making a reference to how Jesus described the experience of trusting in Him in the new testament, Matthew 11:28-30

This is difficult to believe, I know. You have worked very hard your whole life to be at peace, to simply live without hatred and fear. But your journey will always be a difficult and winding road until you let go of your belief that you can transform yourself. A path that relies on "personal effort" or "following the rules" has been traveled for centuries by millions, even billions, of people. And yet, peace remains tentative at best for mankind. The true (sure) path is narrow, not because few have found it, but because it is only delivered through O.N.E. B.E.I.N.G. I know that this seems harsh and unfair for those who have never known God through J.E.S.U.S. C.H.R.I.S.T. and for those who live in parts of the world where the very mention of "Christ" is against the law. The Father has set a timetable for all people that gives each an opportunity, multiple opportunities in fact, to take the W.A.Y. He is waiting for you to rely on Him more than you rely on yourself, and the rate and speed at which people are willing to do this is inter-related and inter-dependent upon their choices to this point. He wishes for everyone to come to Him and waits for the "time" when all are able to turn to Him. That time has come. Come home by way of the S.O.N. and find **R.E.S.T.**

R.E.S.T.: Resonate Energetically in the Sanctity of Truth

Chapter 9: Peace

G.O.O.D.: God's Omnipresent, Omnipotent Domain
S.O.N.: Spirit Offered in Neutrality
P.E.A.C.E.: Predominating Energy with Acceptance of Christ Eternally
L.O.V.E.: Light Over Vibrational Energy
B.E.I.N.G.: Benevolent Entity Interred in Neutral G.O.O.D.
A.B.L.E.: Abiding in the Benevolent Light of Eternity
S.A.V.I.O.R.: Spirit Abiding Vibrational Incarnation to Overcome Rebellion
O.T.H.E.R.: Omnipresent Transmissions Heating/Hating Emmanuel's Resonance
W.A.Y.: Wavelength Abiding in Yahweh/You
J.E.S.U.S.: Jehovah's Eternal Spirit Under/Unified in the S.O.N.
C.H.R.I.S.T.: Consecrated, Holy, Resonating and Indwelling Spirit of Truth
O.N.E.: Omnipresent, Neutral, Eternal
R.E.S.T.: Resonate Energetically in the Sanctity of Truth

PART 2

Being L.O.V.E.

"For everyone who asks receives;
the O.N.E. who seeks finds;
and to the O.N.E. who knocks,
the door will be opened."[1]
—Matthew 7:8

A Word of Encouragement from the Scribe

It is said that when we think of something beautiful, our minds project that image onto our brains. What we "see" internally is dependent upon our ability to remember the details of an image we have seen in the world. Sometimes we are able to imagine an entirely new image, one that has not been made manifest. This type of sight comes from another source in our being—a source that is linked to creativity. When God creates, He imagines what can be and then constructs what *is* through sheer force of His will. His W.I.L.L. is a powerful wind, like a tornado of energy that conjoins natural elements into matter through time and space. His power comes from being L.O.V.E.

The energy of L.O.V.E. is completely life sustaining and always G.O.O.D. for the creation (universe). But our creativity does not spring from the same source. Our ability to "see" what our creations will accomplish is limited to our imagination of their purpose in the world and to our perspective and understanding of our world. His is not limited. The Father's sight is endless. It endures forever and transcends all things (good and bad) so that what is created by the Father is always above the realm of potentiality and within the realm of prosperity. His love is unchangeable, unwavering, unending.

Although I am just a scribe in this process, I am compelled to tell you a bit about my own struggle to understand. When this assignment arrived and the opportunity to say "yes" was presented to me, I willingly and enthusiastically jumped in because of what I can only describe as "supernatural events" prior to the writing of these words. Because of all I had experienced, I thought I needed to ask for additional "sight" for the purpose of seeing beyond the veil and being able to identify the energetic enemy in our midst. But that is not the way to *know* Him. He wants us to come to Him by *faith*. So, He has not granted me this request. I am beginning to understand (K.N.O.W., not think) that I was asking for less, and therefore giving me less than what He intends is not manifesting.

If I stop and be still and allow His influence to guide me, I am taken to places where physical sight is irrelevant. My experiences are not and have never been dependent upon what I have seen, but rather they are a product of what I have known. Now, as time grows faster and His presence comes closer, I am realizing that His call has been to awaken me to the knowing that I have possessed all along. Suspicion has become experience. Experience has become confirmation. Confirmation has become action. Action has become *re-membering* who we really are. Accepting His L.O.V.E. as a means of transforming my current state of being into an eternal state of bliss is what I need to do to re-member and become anchored to the eternal life promised so long ago.

We all have this attachment to His L.O.V.E. inside of us—buried deep in our hearts and waiting to be realized in our minds. The breach we have endured for so long is not related to our own eyesight, but rather to the division between inner knowing and outer evidence—the things we trust because they can be verified by observation (sight). Science has been slowly revealing the truth that lies beyond our vision. Evidence of matter we cannot see has been revealed in every corner of the universe. **So, the real question is what do we K.N.O.W. that cannot be measured? What do we understand that cannot be seen? How does our ability to "see" interfere with our ability to "know"?**

When God calls you to come into His presence, He takes you on a journey that is bereft of sight. There is no visual evidence of His presence. However, it is hard to ignore the way His presence makes you feel. People say that once they accepted Christ, they *knew* they were being changed because they felt different. There is no visual or physical evidence of this change, except perhaps through our ability to observe their change in attitude or behavior. And yet, they insist that they have been "reborn" (re-made) in some meaningful way. I have come to understand that what they know is not a belief, but rather something beyond the constraints of belief. It is a way of being that feels like relief (re-life) to each person who experiences it. Knowing in this way comes with an ability to access a state of being that is grounded in grace, acceptance, peace, and tranquility. It is the first step on the path to becoming L.O.V.E. It is also the first step into a new world, a network of energy that supports knowing that you are now operating under a different set of rules—a construct that is beyond the observable, explainable, verifiable nature of our material world.

If you want to experience this type of knowing, there is only one W.A.Y., one path, one process that leads to it. Acceptance of God's gifts—beginning with the O.N.E. who is A.B.L.E. to take you from darkness to light and, in the process, transform your being into a new creation that is defined by L.O.V.E. (the most powerful source of creation) rather than one that is attached to the energies that form the construct of the observable world. This "in-sight" only comes from letting go of what you can see and allowing that which cannot be seen to enter your being. So, my advice is to try Him. Come to the Father through the S.O.N. and experience the unbreakable, unending, enduring, everlasting state of being called L.O.V.E.

Being L.O.V.E.

The goal of every person on planet earth is to become L.O.V.E. The way to become L.O.V.E. is achieved through a narrow gate, but it is an easy opening to find if you are seeking God with your whole heart and ignoring the temptations produced by the mind. Once through the gate, the process of becoming L.O.V.E. is generous, the way of L.O.V.E. (bandwidth) is wide, and every person who dwells in the L.O.R.D.'s spirit is given G.R.A.C.E. That means that each person finds the way back to P.E.A.C.E. and R.E.S.T. instantaneously because God has already forgiven their actions before they have occurred. The time it takes for our action and God's reaction to interact with one another may make "peace" seem slow to come. But in actuality, it is already in motion before any act that can violate that "peace" is committed. The intensity and degree of suffering for any action we commit is enhanced by our own personal willpower, which we choose to enact independently without guidance and protection from God.

This is how it works: If you are feeling overwhelmed by something and allow it to build within you to a boiling point, chances are that you will act upon the emotion you feel inside. If you do, you will be acting in accord (plucking a chord) within your own power source. Your actions will likely include speaking negatively about someone or something aloud at some point in time. Before you have spoken aloud, the Father knows your intention, and unless you are abiding in **H.I.M.** through the bridge provided by the S.O.N., grace is not automatically granted.

H.I.M.: Holy Immanuel Manifested

But, when you are in H.I.M. and He is in you, your ability to damage yourself is reduced by G.R.A.C.E.

He takes the negative energy you create and dismantles its power to damage both you *and the world around you*. Together, you are being L.O.V.E. and healing is easy because you are *continually* healed. During the process of transformation (becoming L.O.V.E.), it may seem as though healing takes time. But as you grow closer to God (physically, mentally, emotionally, intellectually, and spiritually), any distance or T.I.M.E. between feeling and healing is minimized.

This is why it was possible for Jesus to heal people instantaneously—His relationship with the Father was as close as any H.U.M.A.N. being can come to K.N.O.W. God. In this state of being, L.O.V.E. knows no time, no distance.

For those outside of G.R.A.C.E., prayer is the only means of finding some measure of peace. God sends peace to those who cry out for compassion, but the process of being L.O.V.E. is not in motion continually. Until you have accepted the gift of G.R.A.C.E. through faith in God's S.O.N., you are not plugged into His network. As long as you are grounded in the competing network, healing typically takes place in moments of suffering, and in response to seeking. Once you are in His arms, healing takes place automatically, simultaneously, and continually. Why is there any difference? **Because being L.O.V.E. occurs for those individuals** who have voluntarily given their personal will-power to C.H.R.I.S.T. and, in its place, accepted His W.I.L.L. over their own.

This is important to understand because it is *our will* that creates the opposing forces in our lives, the energy that fights with God's healing power. When we try to fix ourselves, or when we become angry with another person and refuse to forgive and forget whatever has happened, we give those thoughts power and energy to remain in us and in the world. We generate waves of negativity that compete with L.O.V.E., and in the process we endure the physical, mental, and emotional effects of our own negativity. **Without God there to take it from us, it comes back on us.**

Chapter 10: Being Love

L.O.V.E.: Light Over Vibrational Energy

G.R.A.C.E.: God's Resonating Alliance in C.H.R.I.S.T Eternal

P.E.A.C.E.: Predominating Energy with Acceptance of Christ Eternally

R.E.S.T.: Resonate Energetically in the Sanctity of Truth

H.I.M.: Holy Immanuel Manifested

S.O.N.: Spirit Offered in Neutrality

T.I.M.E.: Temporal Insights Meted in Eternity

H.U.M.A.N.: His Ultimate Manifestation Abiding in Neutrality

K.N.O.W.: Know No O.T.H.E.R. Way/Wavelength

O.T.H.E.R.: Omnipresent Transmissions Heating/Hating Emmanuel's Resonance

C.H.R.I.S.T.: Consecrated, Holy, Resonating and Indwelling Spirit of Truth

W.I.L.L.: Word and Intention in L.I.F.E. and L.O.V.E

L.I.F.E.: Light Inside the Fabric of Eternity

CHAPTER 11

Prayer

Prayer is the means given to us to achieve a personal, direct relationship with the living God. It is not a tool of self-reflection or "meditation" as some would believe. It is more than a quiet moment. It's an active conversation with God. The power of **P.R.A.Y.E.R.** is undeniable.

P.R.A.Y.E.R.: Protected/Personal Resonance Aligned with Yahweh's Eternal Resonance

---

I could tell you about thousands of answered prayers, but I'd rather take this opportunity to tell you about how prayer is designed and why it is the means to provide us with our every need.

When God gave man dominion over the earth, He provided a way for two B.E.I.N.G.s united in the energy of L.O.V.E. to cooperatively participate in the growth and experience of the creation. In each instance of co-creation there was a united mind—a telepathic type of conversation. It was a collaboration that took place prior to the manifestation of whatever was desired. God's perspective was required to "vet" the ideas generated because man's perspective was limited and therefore incomplete in its knowledge of the potential impacts of adding to the creation. Man's knowledge of what is added and what it might or might not accomplish is still limited today, and always will be in comparison to what God knows. When the F.A.L.L. of man occurred, God withdrew to a more distant state of being, but did not completely leave the conversation. Man's downfall created a state of being that was different than the state of being required to be in God's presence. So, with several degrees of separation now in place, the conversation could only take place through a device that could penetrate from our state of being to His. Voilà. P.R.A.Y.E.R.

Our minds are capable of thinking great things, which is why we give them such an honored role in our existence. But it's our heart's intelligence that generates the power to co-create. Without God's energy of L.O.V.E. (the energy of the Giver), we cannot push our desires into the cosmos. God answers prayers that are heartfelt, sincere, and good for our state of being. When we pray with heartfelt intention, we push our deepest desires into His realm of creativity, and God responds in kind, with a wave of creativity that reverberates. He mirrors our desires by sending them back to us in the form of pure potential. It's up to us to harness that potential and translate it into something positive in our lives and in our world. **But let me be clear about one thing— your potential to manifest a new world, a new state of being, or anything that was not already created before our separation from God's state of being is extremely limited. What we are granted in our present condition is limited to our own personal growth.** The resources given to us on this planet were put in place eons ago and cannot be altered (except for the destruction we create through our actions). Our resources are finite, and our ability to change them is limited. However, our desire to return to God and a means of changing our own being back into what was originally designed are available through P.R.A.Y.E.R.

You see, "prayer" is often seen as a form of requesting something from God. But in actuality, it is not about asking for things. It's about transformation—of our own beings into something that is capable of withstanding one another and the world we live in and ultimately overcoming the separation syndrome. God resides in us when we *invite* Him to do so. When His Spirit is present, we can receive His G.R.A.C.E., His blessings, and His transformative power in our lives—through transformation in our hearts and minds *first*. As we become Lovers (Givers), the process of co-creation is enhanced through a form of mutual cooperation. P.R.A.Y.E.R. is the means for this transformation—from isolation to partnership and cooperation to collaboration. It's that simple. Use prayer to get to know God within you. **By the way, you are not a "god-man" until God is in you. And even then, you are unable to act alone, or without God's intention and influence.** You are actually two beings that cooperatively create in harmony and L.O.V.E. God is the Giver, and humanity is a manifestation of His **U.N.I.T.Y.**

U.N.I.T.Y.: Undying Neutral and Infinite Truth in Yahweh/You

He transforms you into a Lover (Giver), and your desires become based in Love-centered creation (that which gives before it receives). As you are transformed, your P.R.A.Y.E.R.s become more and more heartfelt, pushing pure L.O.V.E. and loving intentions into the cosmos, where

God responds by sending back (mirroring) your every heart's desire. You are simply required to co-operate with that process to receive all of its benefits, including getting everything your heart truly desires. A heart that has been transformed by God becomes a person who has God's heart for G.O.O.D. And God loves working with people who are after His own heart.

I wish I could tell those of you who are reluctant to surrender your own willpower to God that we could accomplish anything permanent on our own, but it's simply not true. It's not the way things are by design. You can continue to struggle and put all of your effort into making your own way if you want to. God gave us free will to choose—our way or the W.A.Y. When we choose our way, we only look like we are making progress because we are moving stuff around to create the illusion of creating good things through self-promotion and self-reliance. And it's a deceptively good-looking game because we can use the materials given to us to rebuild and to alter that which is already present—making things seem shiny and new. But, in reality, we cannot manifest anything **N.E.W.** without God's involvement.

N.E.W.: Neutral Eternal W.A.Y.

So, you may ask, what about rich and powerful people who seem to get everything they want? Most of the time, powerful people take what they want and get it by stealing or controlling or using the labor of their fellow men. God does not control us, nor does He use people to get what He wants. If God seems to give powerful people who don't know Him (or barely know Him) success in life, it is for the benefit of O.T.H.E.R.s that He does so. This is a tough thing to understand, but again, God's perspective on how things unfold in time and space is vastly superior to our point of view. He takes the long view; we can only see the short one. He moves people and governments and weather around for the benefit of the whole planet. He compels people to seek Him, to do His bidding, and to follow His guidance. And sometimes, if they refuse to acknowledge His presence in their lives, He brings them to their **K.N.E.E.s**

K.N.E.E.s: Kinetic Network of E.V.I.L.'s Energies

His plan for the redemption of mankind was set in motion so long ago that we cannot even comprehend the series of events that are unfolding over T.I.M.E. because our individual lifetimes are so short by design. **But in the grand scheme of things, godless people who appear to be rich and powerful are not in control of what they have and, in fact, are much more in danger of losing it all than those of us who simply wish to know God and to have the power of His presence in our lives.** So, remember this: If you ever thought God somehow lost control, you'd be wrong. He's just bringing us home by the long road and, along the way, allowing us a variety of opportunities to choose how and when we will come H.O.M.E. Since He's ultimately in control, why not take a short cut and just let Him live in you? Give Him your heart and ask Him to transform you by His power and G.R.A.C.E. ... and get H.O.M.E. faster.

Chapter 11: Prayer

P.R.A.Y.E.R.: Protected/Personal Resonance Aligned with Yahweh's Eternal Resonance
B.E.I.N.G.: Benevolent Entity Interred in Neutral G.O.O.D.
L.O.V.E.: Light Over Vibrational Energy
F.A.L.L.: Forbidden Access to L.O.V.E.'s Light
G.R.A.C.E.: God's Resonating Alliance in C.H.R.I.S.T Eternal
C.H.R.I.S.T.: Consecrated, Holy, Resonating and Indwelling Spirit of Truth
U.N.I.T.Y.: Undying Neutral and Infinite Truth in Yahweh/You
G.O.O.D.: God's Omnipresent, Omnipotent Domain
W.A.Y.: Wavelength Abiding in Yahweh/You
N.E.W.: Neutral, Eternal W.A.Y.
O.T.H.E.R.: Omnipresent Transmissions Heating/Hating Emmanuel's Resonance
K.N.E.E.: Kinetic Network of E.V.I.L.'s Energy
E.V.I.L.: Energetic Vibrations Inverting L.I.F.E.
L.I.F.E.: Light Inside the Fabric of Eternity
T.I.M.E.: Temporal Insights Meted in Eternity
H.O.M.E.: Holy O.N.E.s Manifesting in Emeth/Eternity
O.N.E.: Omnipresent, Neutral, Eternal

CHAPTER 12

Acknowledgement

In the United States of America, freedom is celebrated with a ferocity that is unparalleled in the W.O.R.L.D. because our freedoms have been forged from "unity" (one Nation under God[1]) and guarded more fiercely than most every other place in the world. When the Father created us, He gave us free will, which is different from freedom as we know it. Our free will is an ability to choose to accept His blessings—or not. We can live our lives in ways that include God's hand on our journey, guiding and leading and even intervening on our behalf when we grant Him the right to do so. The church calls the act of relinquishing your own will "surrendering to God." But this word *surrender* has caused many to doubt the benefits of surrendering because we live in a world where perseverance and ability of our own making are what we believe get us things like security and prosperity. So, let's dispense with the term *surrender* for the moment and talk about what this really is for the sake of those who feel a twinge of "fear" at the mere thought of surrendering their own power to a higher power—even if they know the higher power is in a unique position to help. Instead, let's talk about *acknowledgment*.

---

[1] This is a reference to wording in the United States of America's Pledge of Allegiance

To acknowledge the existence of something is to verify its presence and, depending upon its role, its ability to be either a positive or a negative influence in your life. Correct? Once you recognize anything, you have acknowledged it on some level, albeit recognition alone is not the fullest expression of acknowledgment. When you fully acknowledge that something is good or bad or works or does not work, you have reached a point in your experience with that particular thing in your life to "place it" accordingly. For example, fire that burns you is dangerous. Fire that cooks your food is beneficial. Setting up circumstances to prevent burning down your home is acknowledged to be a smart and helpful thing for your life's happiness. Eventually, we all find ourselves deciding whether something or someone in our lives is working (beneficial) or not (detrimental).

Christ says...

*I Am not detrimental in any way for anyone who chooses to know Me personally and intimately. Those who keep Me at a "distance" cannot know Me in a way that allows them to acknowledge the power of My presence in their lives. They simply do not have the experience with Me directly to be able to acknowledge and verify My ability as L.O.R.D. and **S.A.V.I.O.R.** to help them live more peaceful, prosperous lives.*

S.A.V.I.O.R.-2: Sanctified Above Vibrational Interference and Operating in Resonance[2]

---

[2] This is the second meaning behind the acronym for the word "Savior"—the first referring to His purpose and the second referring to His ongoing role (in eternity).

And many times, their definition of prosperity aligns with the world's view and definition of it, which differs dramatically from My own. That is not to say that money and security are not essential to human life at this time. But they are not meaningful in terms of eternal well-being. Eternal life comes through transformation. Transformation comes through Me. So those who "surrender" are really just saying, "Your will and not my own." What that means is that those who are giving Me authority in their lives are trusting that I am G.O.O.D., that I am A.B.L.E., and that I will guide them to places of safety for their eternal well-being. Sometimes that journey is a rough one because despite surrendering, the habit of making your own decisions is strong enough to interfere with My guidance. When those who surrender fail to seek My guidance, I can only observe their choices. **Unless and until they come to Me for guidance, I cannot redeem them from bad choices.** *So "surrender" does not mean complete abdication of your own path.* **Surrender is really an acknowledgment of "knowing" I Am present/pre-sent and able to intervene at all times.** *It is still up to each person to turn to Me in each moment. I provide help in the form of understanding, healing, discernment, wisdom, and, ultimately, faith. These all lead to Truth (recognition of the sure way forward).*

In the end, all will be revealed as it is, not as mankind wishes it to be. So, for those who have acknowledged My presence, there is recognition of what works for their highest and best good. For those seeking other sources, or relying on their own effort, I am not present in a way that leads to truth because they have not acknowledged My ability over their own. If you are committed to seeking on your own and resist the opportunity to acknowledge My presence, which in turn opens doors that cannot be opened without My doing, then you are opening doors that are not of My making and may not be beneficial to your life experience. They are temporary (temporal) at best and have nothing to do with My Father's intention for your eternal life.

Remember, the way is narrow for a reason ... there are false passages and temptations at every turn because the W.O.R.L.D. has allowed the delusion of self-reliance to dominate your perceptions. The perception that I Am is not present, that I Am un-A.B.L.E. or unwilling is completely false. The persistent adherence to such a view perpetuates that which is temporary, and in turn, temptation to fall into dis-belief (distance from true L.I.F.E.) wins the day. But My Truth/W.A.Y. will win the war. The easiest way to be on the winning side of the war against E.V.I.L. (the opposition of everlasting L.I.F.E.) is to find your way to the only path that leads to unity. And the Father has willed that it only comes through **M.E.**

M.E.: Manifest Eternity

Chapter 12: Acknowledgment

W.O.R.L.D.: War Of Rebellion in L.O.V.E.'s Domain
L.O.V.E.: Light Over Vibrational Energy
L.O.R.D.: L.O.V.E. Overtaking Rebellious Domains
S.A.V.I.O.R.-2: Sanctified Above Vibrational Interference and Operating in Resonance
G.O.O.D.: God's Omnipresent, Omnipotent Domain
A.B.L.E.: Abiding in the Benevolent Light of Eternity
L.I.F.E.: Light Inside the Fabric of Eternity
W.A.Y.: Wavelength Abiding in Yahweh/You
E.V.I.L.: Energetic Vibrations Inverting L.I.F.E.
M.E.: Manifest Eternity

CHAPTER 13

Knowing

Temptation comes in many forms. Sometimes it is a simple thought of disbelief or doubt. At other times, it is a strong pull to act on an urge that seems to draw you closer and closer, like a moth to a flame. Temptation can be good or bad. It is often defined in the negative, as though only bad things are calling out to you, inviting you to potentially harmful experiences. But the truth is, God is calling out to you, too. He uses every means available to get your attention.

As you read these pages, He is asking you to consider the possibility that your life's path to this point is not a seemingly random series of your own choices, but rather a series of desires—some ruled by your heart and others by your mind. You see, the mind/heart split that occurred at the F.A.L.L. of man brought with it competing desires in addition to competing energies. Your heart already wants what God has willed for you—only good things that bring peace to your life. But your mind wants to control the timing and the nature of everything that comes into your state of being. It tempts you to *think* before **K.N.O.W.I.N.G.**

K.N.O.W.I.N.G.: Kinetic Neurons Oscillating Within and Interred in Neutral G.O.O.D.[1]

It asks you to consider your options—to decide (de-side) from the heart's intentions and make your own will the master of your destiny. Following God's W.I.L.L. for you is not a problem for those who have surrendered their will to the Father's. It becomes easy to receive His guidance when the temptation to think on your own is removed and the heart's intelligence (God's intention) is empowered. Those who seek Him first have a willing heart, one that is strong enough to overpower the temptation of the mind. It is not a condition of the heart to feel *less* than God's intention for you, but it is a condition of separation (being in the W.O.R.L.D.) to believe that less is available to you.

As you give your mind to God (your heart is already programmed for Him), you experience desires that compel you to choose L.O.V.E. over everything else. Working hard to think about love is not the same as simply *being* L.O.V.E. Knowing in your heart that all is well is very different than believing all is well. God wants you to K.N.O.W. Him, not just believe in Him. There is a huge difference between these two approaches. And, K.N.O.W.I.N.G. only comes through the kind of submission to transformation that is permanently installed in both heart and mind. You are already more than halfway there if you believe in love, in goodness, in peace, in being at one with "the universe." You are just one step short of K.N.O.W.I.N.G. it.

---

[1] This is the expanded meaning of K.N.O.W. (To Know No Other Way, or wavelength) and refers to a mind that is actually aligned and co-operating with God. It is the experience of the energetic reality of a mind transformed by God.

Come to the Father through the avenue provided by His S.O.N. (the energetic bridge of transformation that only Christ Jesus can deliver). Stop worrying about being good enough, trying harder to be at peace, trying to love those around you who bring pain and suffering into your world, and start K.N.O.W.I.N.G. the L.O.V.E. of God in your life. As children of the Most High, you are invited to become L.O.V.E., but only those who K.N.O.W. how to be L.O.V.E. are able to come into the joy of the Lord's presence, and only those who have been *permanently* altered to abide within His kingdom (the presence of L.O.V.E. at the highest level) are enabled (in-ability) to co-create in L.O.V.E.—the most powerful wavelength of creation and the one that delivers all that the H.E.A.R.T. desires.

The next time that you are tempted to try something on your own, listen to your heart's desire *first*. What does the intelligence in your heart-center say to you? Don't think about what you believe; pray that God will reveal His intention to you and ask that you K.N.O.W. what that intention is in a way that is beyond doubt, beyond "belief." Is it to strive and to work for His affection and protection? Or is it to simply *be* in His presence? To be still and know I Am?[2] Ask Him to reveal His L.O.V.E. within you and wait for His answer. **Expect the answer to come.** If you seek Him with all of your heart and mind, you will find the True (sure) answer. Once you K.N.O.W. that answer, simply accept it. You will be guided to follow the gift of His instruction—directions that only He can give you. This instruction will stop allowing your mind to take control of the process. "Knowing" God is only possible through K.N.O.W.I.N.G. His

---

[2] This is a reference to scripture, specifically Psalms 46:10. "Be still and know that I Am God."

true intention for you, and the only way His intentions come into being is through the bridge He has constructed, which is directly connected to Him in a way that we are not. Christ Jesus is the only O.N.E. who has proven Himself worthy of abiding at the highest level (at the right hand). It is through the S.O.N. that the Father provides answers. Accept His S.O.N. and you are accepting the only direct connection that God has extended to those living in darkness. Do not be tempted to accept instruction from any other source for you will find it to be temporary at best, and misleading (missed-leading) at worst. Those who seek guidance in the wrong places are subjected to great torment and mental anguish. Deception abounds in places where "guides" are actively pursuing the mind of man for their own purposes (which we will discuss later). In the meantime, find the True way (sure W.A.Y.) by praying for His L.O.V.E. to enter your life and then listening for His response. After that, it's up to you. Will you decide (de-side)? Will you remember (re-member)?

Chapter 13: Knowing

F.A.L.L.: Forbidden Access to L.O.V.E.'s Light

L.O.V.E.: Light Over Vibrational Energy

K.N.O.W.I.N.G.: Kinetic Neurons Oscillating Within and Interred in Neutral G.O.O.D.

G.O.O.D.: God's Omnipresent, Omnipotent Domain

W.I.L.L.: Word and Intention in L.I.F.E. and L.O.V.E

L.I.F.E.: Light Inside the Fabric of Eternity

W.O.R.L.D.: War Of Rebellion in L.O.V.E.'s Domain

K.N.O.W.: Know No O.T.H.E.R. Way/Wavelength

O.T.H.E.R.: Omnipresent Transmissions Heating/Hating Emmanuel's Resonance

S.O.N.: Spirit Offered in Neutrality

H.E.A.R.T.: Heaven's Eternal Alliance Resonating Truth

O.N.E.: Omnipresent, Neutral, Eternal

W.A.Y.: Wavelength Abiding in Yahweh/You

CHAPTER 14

Denial

Once upon a time there was a princess who went looking for love in all of the wrong places. She was sent on a journey, only to discover that those seeking physical pleasure and satisfaction in worldly things were being held prisoner by the very things they acquired and coveted in their lives. On her journey, she met many good people who, despite displaying their admiration for her, could not really love her with all of their hearts. They were compromised inside and in denial of their own condition. The more they sought satisfaction in the world, the more they hurt the princess's heart. It pained her to see that they could not be truthful with her, nor could they be loyal companions. Each tried to commit to the light and love she sought to bring into their lives, but in the end, each submitted to their own desires and betrayed the princess in ways that brought her great sadness. Try as she might, her light was not strong enough to help them see that their worldly tendencies were slowly killing them, and that their hearts wanted to be free from the pain and suffering each was causing in their own lives. In the end, she could only pray for their release from bondage to the W.O.R.L.D.

If you are having people problems (like our princess) and are continually seeking a life filled with love and joy and peace, I suggest that you stop expecting broken people to be able to be the source of the happiness you seek and start looking to God for the healing that only He can bring. Continually believing in humanity's capacity to love more than the presence of God's L.O.V.E. is to remain in **D.E.N.I.A.L.**

D.E.N.I.A.L.: Damaging Energies/Entities Negating Infinity's Alliance with L.O.V.E.

Humans have traveled the road of D.E.N.I.A.L. for millennia, searching for a path that would allow the kind of love and light that is offered by good people to prevail in a world filled with darkness. But, the light of "good people" has been compromised or weakened by the darkness to which they were subjected every day. The pull of the world's network is very strong. It seems as though we can overcome it by being "good" and doing what is "right," following society's rules and living righteous lives. But without God's intervention in our lives, our B.E.I.N.G.s are subject to transgression and, ultimately, despair. Without God, there is no hope of renewal in the way that is needed for permanent transformation from dark to light. Even the best, most godly people cannot help you become L.O.V.E. Only God's H.A.N.D. on our life's path can change us from what we all are into what He intended for us to be—co-creators filled with the light of His L.O.V.E. and A.B.L.E. to accomplish our every heart's desire using the energy of His L.O.V.E. to make it manifest. **The number-one reason that we continue to struggle is because we cannot recognize that we are all in D.E.N.I.A.L.**

We want so badly to believe that babies are born innocent and that mankind is essentially good and capable of self-improvement. We hold fast to the idea that over time evolution contains the power to make us capable of greater love and to permanently produce a more compassionate species of human being through the survival of those predicated by acts of love—and that knowledge of evil and doing bad things to one another will eventually cease because somehow good people will prevail. We talk about "love" having the power to prevail over darkness, and we are taught that love conquers all. We believe that if we are "good enough," someday mankind will be brought out of darkness for all of eternity and live in peace and harmony without the continuing threat of evil destroying everything we have accomplished. It is a noble and admirable quest, a lovely dream, a seemingly harmless path if taken with the best intentions. **It is also the greatest distraction known to man.**

If we believe that we are capable of re-creating our own human nature, then we have fallen into the trap designed by the opposing network to keep us prisoners in the fallen world. It is not your fault that this network exists. It is not your fault that your nature was compromised by it so long ago. It is not your personal doing (or undoing) that has left the world in this karmic loop of self-reliance. **It's a design that we are born into.** Stop denying the power of the world's pull in your life and recognize that only a higher power can overcome it. Denial of God's power to heal the world and everything in it is what *keeps* us prisoner. Breaking free from this energetic prison (cycle) of temptation and pain requires submission to an authority that is greater than each of us, greater than the world's (nature's) ability to heal, and greater than all other forces known (and unknown) by mankind. The only force strong enough to overcome the world is the O.N.E. **B.O.R.N.** for that purpose.

B.O.R.N.: Begat in Omnipotent
Residence/Resonance of Neutrality

The O.N.E. made for redemption of the world came to overcome it, not to judge it. God sent His S.O.N. in human form to re-seed the world with the spirit of His L.O.V.E. and, in the process, to anchor it here for all to use to escape the prison of our own limitations. We cannot overcome, no matter how good, how disciplined, how faithful to doing "right" we are. It is not a matter of effort on our part; it is a matter of breaking free from our "inmate" design and the power of the network that makes up our world's design (prison). It's a network of limitation that we, through no fault of our own, are born into. Our design was compromised, and therefore the world's as well, long before you were ever conceived (willed into matter).

The only way to overcome this reality is to acknowledge it. D.E.N.I.A.L. is not a useful state of being if you are seeking L.O.V.E. D.E.N.I.A.L. does not help you become L.O.V.E. D.E.N.I.A.L. only prolongs finding the True (sure) path and increases the potential for agony to eventually catch up to you. It is not enough to *want* to change. It is not enough to believe you *can* change. It is not enough to pray to God to change you, without also surrendering your entire being to *be changed*. And, the only path of change offered is through the acceptance of the O.N.E. sent for this purpose. J.E.S.U.S. C.H.R.I.S.T. is the means, the bridge, the light, the life, the way home.

If you do not think (K.N.O.W.) that permanent peace of mind and heart is possible, then I recommend that you ask a Christian who has been changed by C.H.R.I.S.T. into a new being. Yes, I am talking about someone who has been re-

B.O.R.N. by the power of God's S.O.N. dwelling within them. Don't let the concept of being "born again" and what you may think you know about it keep you from investigating the Truth (the sure path).

It is not God's intention that anyone who believes in Him be misled by any person or by any religious order. It was also not His intention that mankind learn of Christ's purpose and mission through the prism of religion. We have been given the ability to simply ignore the constructs of "faith" as defined by the world's churches and reach out directly to God's S.O.N. for the kind of healing that is granted through God Himself. In our searching, we have come to think (believe) that being a Christian means doing right and living by a particular religious doctrine. **But, any system of belief that requires your participation in ritual, or submission to its law and rule, is trying to take the place (the space) between you and God's S.O.N. that is provided to *anyone* who asks Him to come into their heart and live within them for the purpose of transformation.** The world wants you to deny this possibility. God wants you to acknowledge that **H.E. I.S. A.B.L.E.**

H.E. I.S. A.B.L.E.: Holy Emmanuel's Immanent Source/Spirit Abiding in the Benevolent Light of Eternity

---

Which will you choose? You have been given free will to decide (and de-side) and, thankfully, a heart that is not completely ruled by the opposing network. Take the time to pray about this today and find the answer for yourself, within yourself. God wants you to choose to be changed by Him. He does not wish for you to struggle for the entirety of your life looking for a path that does not exist without His presence. He said, "Seek and you shall find, knock and the door shall be opened."[1] **This moment is a door that is being opened.** Walk through it unashamed and unfettered by your past, because nothing else matters (is made manifest)—only that which is given by God Himself. He gave His S.O.N. so that you could use H.I.M. to come H.O.M.E.

Do not be confused by the idea that you are a "god" who has the ability to manifest what you want in life without God's influence on your life. Remember that God's W.I.L.L. alone provides for every living thing that is made into matter. Take the Father and the S.O.N. and receive the power that will be sent to you in the form of the **H.O.L.Y.** Spirit.

H.O.L.Y.: Heaven's Omnipotent Light in Yahwey/You

---

[1] This is a reference to scripture, specifically Matthew 7:7.

Chapter 14: Denial

W.O.R.L.D.: War Of Rebellion in L.O.V.E.'s Domain

L.O.V.E.: Light Over Vibrational Energy

D.E.N.I.A.L.: Damaging Energies/Entities Negating Infinity's Alliance with L.O.V.E.

B.E.I.N.G.: Benevolent Entity Interred in Neutral G.O.O.D.

G.O.O.D.: God's Omnipresent, Omnipotent Domain

H.A.N.D.: Heaven's Alliance in Neutral Dominion

A.B.L.E.: Abiding in the Benevolent Light of Eternity

O.N.E.: Omnipresent, Neutral, Eternal

B.O.R.N.: Begat in the Omnipotent Residence/Resonance of Neutrality

S.O.N.: Spirit Offered in Neutrality

J.E.S.U.S.: Jehovah's Eternal Spirit Under/Unified in the S.O.N.

C.H.R.I.S.T.: Consecrated, Holy, Resonating and Indwelling Spirit of Truth

K.N.O.W.: Know No O.T.H.E.R. Way/Wavelength

O.T.H.E.R.: Omnipresent Transmissions Heating/Hating Emmanuel's Resonance

H.E. I.S. A.B.L.E.: Holy Emmanuel's Immanent Source/Spirit Abiding in the Benevolent Light of Eternity

H.I.M.: Holy Immanuel Manifested

H.O.M.E.: Holy O.N.E.s Manifesting in Emeth/Eternity

W.I.L.L.: Word and Intention in L.I.F.E. and L.O.V.E

L.I.F.E.: Light Inside the Fabric of Eternity
H.O.L.Y.: Heaven's Omnipotent Light in Yahweh/You

CHAPTER 15

Pushing Back the Dark

The second commandment that the Father issued to His people was to love one another: O.N.E. and O.T.H.E.R.[1] This was a deliberate command, given in a deliberate order for a simple reason. **You are able to overcome darkness by doing this.**

The separation that exists now between God and man is not the only separation occurring. The distance between men was once limited to a physical sensation of separateness, but not an actual separation. When the breach of trust and obedience to the **L.A.W.** (instruction) occurred, the sensation of being at one with all that is was also severed.

L.A.W.: L.O.V.E.'s Abiding Wavelength

So, man's ability to recognize that he is connected to all things was turned from *being* into *feeling*. And, the sensation

---

[1] This is a reference to scripture, specifically Matthew 22: 37-40 where Jesus reaffirms the need to continue to obey the first and second of the ten commandments given to Moses in Old Testament, and how all of the "law" is fulfilled in these two. Here, he is emphasizing the need for us to love one another through the energetic definition of both people in Omnipresent Neutral Energy and people attached to Omnipresent Transmissions Heating/Hating Emmanuel's Resonance.

of separateness feels very real. But the Father **I.S.** and the world **I.S.** and man **I.S.** part of O.N.E. big energetic wavelength called L.O.V.E.

I.S.: Immanent Source/Spirit/Space

Loving one another comes easily for those who love you back. It is not so easy to love people who are trapped in darkness and exhibiting feelings of hatred. But *feelings* are not real compared to *being*. Thought generates emotion. Emotion pushes various wavelengths into your state of mind (separateness). Separation causes feelings of isolation and a desire to protect your own "space." **But your "space" is not really your own.** It is an illusion that begins and ends with your ability to sense (or your lack thereof) the extension of your being into the higher planes of existence and beyond your own body definition. When you connect with another person physically, emotionally, or intellectually, what you are really connecting to is a wavelength that unifies you in *experience*, not feelings. Matter is what gives context to your sensation of separation, but it is not part of your true experience. When you come to the Father for protection, you think that you are coming to ask that nothing interfere with your "space"—the things that belong to you, the dominion that you have carved out for your existence in the world. **However, the truth is that your existence is only partially defined by matter (physicality). Your true self is defined by your relationship to the higher planes.** As you are A.B.L.E. to ascend to the experience of being on a higher plane (mentally, spiritually, emotionally), you are raising your vibrational level of existence, drawing closer to the source of the wavelength of

L.O.V.E. (closer to the Father, the Giver, the Source). When you are A.B.L.E. to love O.T.H.E.R.s as you love God and your "self," you are raising the vibrational level of all that I.S.

You cannot proceed to the highest realms of existence without taking O.T.H.E.R.s along for the ride. Separation is only an illusion, so actively loving those around you benefits *you*. **In fact, it benefits you more than it benefits them.** As a Giver of L.O.V.E., you L.O.V.E. like the Father and are being L.O.V.E. in ways that O.T.H.E.R.s are not. This activity sends a signal to the highest realm, that you are A.B.L.E. In so doing, the Father sends His power back to those whom He **T.R.U.S.T.s**.

T.R.U.S.T.: Truth Resonating in U.N.I.T.Y. with the S.O.N. in T.I.M.E.

The agreement is made to pursue L.O.V.E., to pursue H.I.M., to co-operate with Him in U.N.I.T.Y. for the benefit of all. The all that I.S.

Loving another person, especially one who continually causes pain in your life, is much easier when you realize that the Father wants you to L.O.V.E. without attachment. **He wants you to be more attached to H.I.M. than to the world or anyone and anything in it.** When the focus of your attention and intention shifts to the things of heaven (His realm, the highest realm), you are able to overcome the struggles of the world through *compassionate detachment*. The one/O.N.E. who modeled this for you is the Son/S.O.N. His experience in the world encompassed all that there I.S.—from both the highest realm (heaven) and the lowest (hell) and everything in between. Christ was not spared the experience of the W.O.R.L.D. He experienced betrayal, loss, disappointment, hatred, love, friendship, anxiety, fear, compassion, loyalty, joy, temptation, and every other emotion known to man *by design*. His life was planned, and His path was set in motion by the Father for the purpose of understanding and overcoming our experience of separation. His life was lived for the express purpose of showing us *how to overcome*. When you read about how He handled each person—those who lied to Him, betrayed Him, feared for their safety when with Him—you realize that His response to each experience was *compassionate detachment*. He guided, instructed, and led through displays of compassion. He kept His emotional distance from the negative feelings that bombarded Him—in each case, to prevent the type of attachments that the W.O.R.L.D. generates from becoming a part of His B.E.I.N.G. here. And when He felt the presence of F.E.A.R., He turned to the Father for strength and gave up His own will in favor of the W.I.L.L. of the O.N.E. who sent Him.[2]

When you hear someone say Christ lived a perfect life, do not take that to mean one without pain or even one without the continual threat of S.I.N. His B.E.I.N.G. was continually targeted and assaulted with the wavelengths of those around Him, just as you are. His purpose was to R.I.S.E. above those attachments and live without becoming compromised by the world's condition.

His story (history) was designed to show us the way forward while we are here. One day the conditions we live in will be forever changed, and the veil of separation will be lifted for all to see the Truth (W.A.Y.). But until that day comes, you are best served when you serve O.T.H.E.R.s in

---

[2] The most famous example of Christ giving up His will for the Father's was in the Garden of Gethsemane just before His arrest and crucifixion: Matthew 26:39.

the spirit of L.O.V.E. Connect to the O.N.E. who was sent, lived, died, and rose above the W.O.R.L.D.'s condition for the instruction and strength needed to overcome. Accept C.H.R.I.S.T. in your heart and mind and *be* the way forward.

Chapter 15: Pushing Back The Dark

O.N.E.: Omnipresent, Neutral, Eternal

O.T.H.E.R.: Omnipresent Transmissions Heating/Hating Emmanuel's Resonance

L.A.W.: L.O.V.E.'s Abiding Wavelength

I.S.: Immanent Source/Spirit/Space

L.O.V.E.: Light Over Vibrational Energy

A.B.L.E.: Abiding in the Benevolent Light of Eternity

T.R.U.S.T.: Truth Resonating in U.N.I.T.Y. with the S.O.N. in T.I.M.E

U.N.I.T.Y.: Undying Neutral and Infinite Truth in Yahweh/You

S.O.N.: Spirit Offered in Neutrality

T.I.M.E.: Temporal Insights Meted in Eternity

H.I.M.: Holy Immanuel Manifested

W.O.R.L.D.: War Of Rebellion in L.O.V.E.'s Domain

B.E.I.N.G.: Benevolent Entity Interred in Neutral G.O.O.D.

G.O.O.D.: God's Omnipresent, Omnipotent Domain

F.E.A.R.: Foreign Energy Altering Reality

W.I.L.L.: Word and Intention in L.I.F.E. and L.O.V.E

L.I.F.E.: Light Inside the Fabric of Eternity

S.I.N.: Satan's Interfering Network

R.I.S.E.: Reside/Re-side Inside the Sanctity of Eternity

W.A.Y.: Wavelength Abiding in Yahweh/You

CHAPTER 16

Surrender

The world tells us that we are capable of doing great things. And while that is true for most things in our lives, it is not *the* Truth (W.A.Y.) that God intends for His relationship with mankind. To **S.U.R.R.E.N.D.E.R.** is simply to accept that the power of L.O.V.E. is greater than all of the effort any person can muster. In fact, to surrender is divine.

S.U.R.R.E.N.D.E.R.: Salvation Under a Relationship Resonating Eternally in the Neutral Domain of Everlasting Reciprocity

---

To act on one's own accord is quite literally acting against the power coming from the Giver. Why? **Because your own desires, thoughts, dreams, and actions produce opposing forces that compete with the power of L.O.V.E.** It is true. You think you are doing good, acting in accordance with God's will. But what if the Truth (W.A.Y.) to really *be* good is to surrender all self-initiated acts and simply allow God to refine you and reshape you? Do you believe that this is possible? If not, that is your first stumbling block.

The only way to get past the perception of impossibility is to defy the thought that you are more capable than God.

Realize that your capabilities (abilities that have been capped) are limited. His are not. If you open your heart willingly to the power of God's L.O.V.E. transformation in your life, body, spirit, experience, "being" becomes a simpler matter (manifestation). Yes—I mean that literally. Your B.E.I.N.G. is transformed from dark to light, from complicated to simple. The competing energies that bind you to the negative forces in nature, and to the helpless and seemingly hopeless conditions in the world, literally disappear because He is A.B.L.E. to produce the kind of change in you that is far more effective than any human capability. He I.S. You are not. But the good news is that through the presence of the S.O.N. in your heart and mind, you can easily become L.O.V.E. You can easily *be like Him.*

C.H.R.I.S.T. brings the Father's L.O.V.E. to us through a unique bond, an energetic connection that is simply not available anywhere else. This is why you must consider the possibility that His W.I.L.L. for us to know Jesus Christ personally was and is without error. It may seem like such a narrow passage cannot possibly be the intention of God Almighty for His children. But, just as the physics of the universe require a specific set of instructions delivered by a few basic elements[1], re-creating anything also requires a unique set of instructions—and a different connection to the source of creation. **C.H.R.I.S.T. is that connection.** The way is narrow for reasons beyond our capabilities to see, to measure,

---

[1] The Holy Spirit's original instruction here specifically stated "four" elements – however, when asking for guidance on whether or not to be that specific here, he allowed me to change this (with the understanding that I would also provide a footnote). The change was allowed to acknowledge that this statement could create dissention and argument, as science does not currently define or agree on which elements or how many are necessary to create life. However, the Spirit has never wavered from the original number of four.

to understand. And we, not knowing with certainty how it works, ask *why*? The answer is simple.

To re-create something originally created by the Father (Giver) without completely destroying it in the process requires surgical procedures, much like surgery that focuses a laser beam onto the object being repaired. In this kind of operation, it would not make any sense to even consider re-creating anything using a broader spectrum of light or a laser beam that is not specifically attuned to the frequency required to heal without disruption of the physical matter surrounding the patient. This is why C.H.R.I.S.T. came in the way He did. **He was surgically implanted in the world, surgically extracted from it, and is precisely re-making those who ask Him to.** So, even the patients are surgically attended to *one at a time*, and each in His own T.I.M.E. It is a personal journey for a reason; it's a personal relationship and commitment to be permanently changed that exists directly between you and Him. And it requires that you S.U.R.R.E.N.D.E.R. your will to His W.I.L.L.

The Father (Giver) sends His healing and transformative wavelength through the S.O.N. He was sent for this work— to change each of us from dark to light, to heal each of us heart and mind, to unify every one for the *return to the O.N.E.*

Are you coming along for the ride? It's free and available to everyone. Or are you going to continue to work on yourself until you have exhausted every other means known to you and tested every other path? Think about it for a minute. We work very hard to change who we are, and we even acknowledge that we need it for a multitude of things. But, is that enough? Is that even the goal? **What if the opportunity to change *what* you are—and not just *how* you act—was the real goal?** Can you re-create yourself? Let that notion go. Give it up. S.U.R.R.E.N.D.E.R.

to the L.O.R.D. J.E.S.U.S. C.H.R.I.S.T.; and then, just be still and K.N.O.W. that He is the O.N.E. who is truly A.B.L.E.

Chapter 16: Surrender

W.A.Y.: Wavelength Abiding in Yahweh/You

S.U.R.R.E.N.D.E.R.: Salvation Under a Relationship Resonating Eternally in the Neutral Domain of Everlasting Reciprocity

L.O.V.E.: Light Over Vibrational Energy

B.E.I.N.G.: Benevolent Entity Interred in Neutral G.O.O.D.

G.O.O.D.: God's Omnipresent, Omnipotent Domain

A.B.L.E.: Abiding in the Benevolent Light of Eternity

I.S.: Immanent Source/Spirit/Space

S.O.N.: Spirit Offered in Neutrality

C.H.R.I.S.T.: Consecrated, Holy, Resonating and Indwelling Spirit of Truth

W.I.L.L.: Word and Intention in L.I.F.E. and L.O.V.E

L.I.F.E.: Light Inside the Fabric of Eternity

L.O.V.E.: Light Over Vibrational Energy

T.I.M.E.: Temporal Insights Meted in Eternity

O.N.E.: Omnipresent, Neutral, Eternal

K.N.O.W.: Know No O.T.H.E.R. Way/Wavelength

O.T.H.E.R.: Omnipresent Transmissions Heating/Hating Emmanuel's Resonance

L.O.R.D.: L.O.V.E. Overtaking Rebellious Domains

J.E.S.U.S.: Jehovah's Eternal Spirit Under/Unified in the S.O.N.

CHAPTER 17

Commitment

When two souls commit to one another in a bond of eternal bliss, there is a change in physical matter. Those two people relate to each other differently than before, with a connection that is unbreakable on several levels of existence. Likewise, mankind is designed to have an unbreakable bond with the **F.A.T.H.E.R.**

F.A.T.H.E.R.: Forever Abiding in the Truth of Heaven's Eternal Resonance/Residence

---

His design was committed to the ether as part of its essence long ago. In the beginning, His intention was to create a world where humans were manifestations of His W.I.L.L., and A.B.L.E. to experience all of the joy He intended. Joy came from His Source alone and His W.I.L.L. was extracted from Source in a seamless stream of unified consciousness. You knew His W.I.L.L. for you, and you acted in accord (on the same wavelength) with it. There was no strife, no struggle, no dissent, only unity and love. His commitment to this design has never wavered. It is your will that has altered the state of B.E.I.N.G. experienced, and the state of G.R.A.C.E. allowed to flow through to the creation to restore it.

When you exert your own intentions, His wavelength of L.O.V.E. is fractured before its arrival in you. You are mirroring your intention back to Source, instead of simply receiving from Source. It is a condition that requires your acceptance of His W.I.L.L. over your own to receive the G.R.A.C.E. needed to alter both you and your experience in the W.O.R.L.D. **His L.O.V.E. has never stopped coming for you. Only your ability to receive it has changed.** This is why His L.O.V.E. never ends--because it never has. Redirection of His L.O.V.E. to another realm has occurred, but you have never stopped it from being sent and He has never stopped sending it.

Do not mistake His redirection of His W.I.L.L. as a withdrawal of His L.O.V.E. from Source, or as punishment of any kind. It is not. His W.I.L.L. must remain at a distance until your W.I.L.L. is unified with Source.

Christ says...

"I Am the way to Source, and through me, all must come to the F.A.T.H.E.R.'s residence in U.N.I.T.Y.[1]"

U.N.I.T.Y.-2: Un-ending Neutrality Interred in Truth and in You

---

The condition of the world is such that renewal for those who choose it is not possible in the world as it is now. However, it is destined to be, in a world where no alternate route to receiving His L.O.V.E. is available. This is not to say

---

[1] This is the second definition of U.N.I.T.Y. and refers to the state of being achieved once Christ has completed His work in you. The first definition of U.N.I.T.Y. (Undying Neutral and Infinite Truth in Yahwey/You) is used to convey the relationship as originally intended for humanity.

that He does not respect free will. If that were true, He would not have granted it in the first place. The changes required to unite mankind in the world condition and prepare those who have **C.H.O.S.E.N.**[2] (of their own free will) to receive His continual L.O.V.E. are destructive to those who have chosen the alternate option.

C.H.O.S.E.N.: Consecrated Holy Ones Seeking Eternal Neutrality

---

The alternative state of being is not peaceful, not joyful, not pain free (physically or mentally).

Christ says...

*"I Am not coming to judge, nor did I come the first time for that purpose. I Am coming to take those who have freely C.H.O.S.E.N. to live in the light of the F.A.T.H.E.R.'S L.O.V.E. to it. His L.O.V.E. light is fractured into particles in the here and now. But in the light of eternity, His L.O.V.E. is a constant stream that flows to each creation in an unbroken, powerful river of L.I.F.E. The difference that people do not seem to understand is that it is **you** who must change residence, not H.I.M. I Am able to take you to the new home created for those who choose to come H.O.M.E.—to a state of peace and joy. What do you choose? Search your heart and ask yourself now. Am I committed to peace, joy, harmony? Or am I committed to chaos, struggle, control?"*

---

[2] The Holy Spirit wishes to convey that this term "chosen" has been manipulated by some to mean that certain persons are "special" or elevated by God for His purposes. He wishes to clarify that everyone who chooses the S.O.N. (Spirit Offered in Neutrality) of their own free will is chosen.

Christ requests that you pause here to really contemplate this question.

"In your present state, your only means of B.E.I.N.G. L.O.V.E. is to be transformed by L.O.V.E. (from H.I.M. through M.E.). If you do not accept this gift of transformation, your only means of pursuing L.O.V.E. is through your own intentions. Although they may be well intended, the physics of your existence do not permit His L.O.V.E. to remain in a permanent way in the world until the world can also receive from Source. Both you and the world must be changed to resonate with Source instead of reflecting your own intention back to it. Healing the world requires destroying what is in place at this time. **Destruction of the world's current vibrational state is part of healing it.** On a very deep level, if you search your heart with all of your B.E.I.N.G., you already know this. The F.A.T.H.E.R. gave each of His creations the option to choose their own path, and this one was chosen for you by a deceitful trick of those sent to protect you. It is not your fault that the condition exists, but because you are part of the wavelength designed to oppose all of L.I.F.E. and also U.N.I.T.Y. in His L.O.V.E., you are trapped in D.E.A.T.H. and destruction **until** you choose to let go of that part of who you are and become something entirely pure and free of the counter-vibrational forces of destruction. He does not wish to destroy His creation, only re-make it for the benefit of those whom He L.O.V.E.s., and in return, have committed their L.O.V.E. to H.I.M. It is your choice. Which will you commit to?"

Chapter 17: Commitment

F.A.T.H.E.R.: Forever Abiding in the Truth of Heaven's Eternal Resonance/Residence

W.I.L.L.: Word and Intention in L.I.F.E. and L.O.V.E

L.I.F.E.: Light Inside the Fabric of Eternity

L.O.V.E.: Light Over Vibrational Energy

A.B.L.E.: Abiding in the Benevolent Light of Eternity

B.E.I.N.G.: Benevolent Entity Interred in Neutral G.O.O.D.

G.O.O.D.: God's Omnipresent, Omnipotent Domain

G.R.A.C.E.: God's Resonating Alliance in C.H.R.I.S.T Eternal

C.H.R.I.S.T.: Consecrated, Holy, Resonating and Indwelling Spirit of Truth

W.O.R.L.D.: War Of Rebellion in L.O.V.E.'s Domain

U.N.I.T.Y.-2: Unending Neutrality Interred in Truth and in You

C.H.O.S.E.N.: Consecrated Holy Ones Seeking Eternal Neutrality

H.I.M.: Holy Immanuel Manifested

H.O.M.E.: Holy O.N.E.s Manifesting in Emeth/Eternity

O.N.E.: Omnipresent, Neutral, Eternal

M.E.: Manifest Eternity

U.N.I.T.Y.: Undying Neutral and Infinite Truth in Yahweh/You

D.E.A.T.H.: Dissonant Energy Altered Through Heat/Hate

CHAPTER 18

Intention

The way is clear for those who intend to follow the path to L.O.V.E. (the Giver). They are less concerned with their own needs than the needs of others, by design. When you intend to put L.O.V.E. first in your heart and mind, you begin to *be* L.O.V.E. by giving of yourself first, and then receiving the love of others in return. L.O.V.E. comes easily between two people who truly care for one another. L.O.V.E. from The F.A.T.H.E.R. comes the same way. If your intention is to be with H.I.M. in every way, on every level, and in every aspect of your existence (B.E.I.N.G.) then your intention and His are aligned. You are A.B.L.E. to receive His L.O.V.E. because your intention and His are the same and the reception is perfectly clear. When your intention is to promote your own desires, or to control your surroundings as a means of protecting yourself in the world, you are on another wavelength and unable to receive His L.O.V.E. from **S.O.U.R.C.E.**

S.O.U.R.C.E.: Sanctified Omnipotent U.N.I.T.Y. Resonating in C.H.R.I.S.T. Eternally

---

It's like being out of phase or hearing static on a radio. When you tune the radio dial to align the internal crystalline reception with the correct frequency, the music comes in loud and clear. **You are like a tuner that is tuned to the wrong wavelength. And the power of your intention is the device you must use to change your station.**

Many have discovered the power of intention. But few have recognized that your own intention does not work in isolation within the universe. After all, it's called a *uni-verse* for a good reason. The resonance of each one of His creations is designed and defined by The F.A.T.H.E.R. in each circumstance. So, rocks resonate differently than trees, and trees differently than people, etc. In each realm (dimension) resonance is aligned to the level of existence for each creation's frequency—and there are many frequencies. But there is only O.N.E. wavelength to receive His L.O.V.E. directly from S.O.U.R.C.E. And all of creation is capable of tuning into it, by choice.

Your intention is the key to moving the needle for yourself, and your world. If it remains your intention to rely on your own effort to make changes in your life and body occur, then you will find (*your will finds*) that your abilities are capped. There is a limit to what you can accomplish on your own. Again, it is not your fault that your abilities are limited. They were "high-jacked" (attached to and taken over) by beings sent to the lowest realms. Using knowledge of this realm that they once possessed at the higher realms, they found a way to use your bodies for their ascension to this realm. They were sent to the *lowest* realm, banished from His presence, to experience the *lowest* form of being for all eternity. But, in the process, their intentions to inhabit this realm and to use your life force as fuel for their existence was unleashed. Unfortunately, it was your own desire to know *all* forms of existence that opened the door for them. Despite this, The F.A.T.H.E.R. never stopped Loving (Giving). His intention never changed. *Yours did.*

But it is easy to change it back! If you understand that His L.O.V.E. never ceases and that *your will* is the only obstacle to receiving the full power of His L.O.V.E., then the only thing left to do is S.U.R.R.E.N.D.E.R. your will and let H.I.M. change your intentions. Many people are frightened by this thought because they lack the ability to trust after all that has happened. This is understandable, and under the circumstances, expected. The world is not trust-worthy. Your fellow man cannot be trusted unless he loves you more than he loves himself. Do you know anyone who can be trusted in this way? Has another ever demonstrated this kind of love for you? If the S.O.N. comes to mind, then you are starting to get the picture.

Christ says...

"I Am sent to show you that the O.N.E. who made you L.O.V.E.s. you to the point of self-sacrifice. I Am. L.O.V.E.s. you to the point of self-destruction. I Am gives of Himself freely and in accordance with The F.A.T.H.E.R.'S W.I.L.L. **I Am He who was sent to deliver you.** *Come through M.E. to The F.A.T.H.E.R. and become a renewed (re-created anew) creation. My F.A.T.H.E.R.'S intention is **all** consuming. If you bring a willing heart to H.I.M., you will be re-created without delay. Once you have accepted His presence in your B.E.I.N.G. and tossed out the interfering power of your own effort (and the counter-productive waves created by your own will), it is impossible for you to remain unchanged. Salvation is simply getting on His wavelength and allowing it to consume your entire B.E.I.N.G. so that you can ascend to a higher frequency than you can raise yourself. Come along for the ride to L.I.F.E.*

I Am waiting to take you **H.O.M.E.**[1]"

H.O.M.E.-2: Holy O.N.E.'s Meeting
in Eternity

---

[1] This is the second definition of H.O.M.E. and is used to describe a literal meeting place that will be made available at the second coming of J.E.S.U.S. C.H.R.I.S.T. (Jehovah's Eternal Spirit Under the S.O.N. as the Consecrated, Holy, Resonating and Indwelling Spirit of Truth).

Chapter 18: Intention

L.O.V.E.: Light Over Vibrational Energy

F.A.T.H.E.R.: Forever Abiding in the Truth of Heaven's Eternal Resonance/Residence

H.I.M.: Holy Immanuel Manifested

B.E.I.N.G.: Benevolent Entity Interred in Neutral G.O.O.D.

G.O.O.D.: God's Omnipresent, Omnipotent Domain

A.B.L.E.: Abiding in the Benevolent Light of Eternity

S.O.U.R.C.E.: Sanctified Omnipotent U.N.I.T.Y. Resonating in C.H.R.I.S.T. Eternally

U.N.I.T.Y.: Undying Neutral and Infinite Truth in Yahweh/You

C.H.R.I.S.T.: Consecrated, Holy, Resonating and Indwelling Spirit of Truth

O.N.E.: Omnipresent, Neutral, Eternal

S.U.R.R.E.N.D.E.R.: Salvation Under a Relationship Resonating Eternally in the Neutral Domain of Everlasting Reciprocity

S.O.N.: Spirit Offered in Neutrality

M.E.: Manifest Eternity

L.I.F.E.: Light Inside the Fabric of Eternity

H.O.M.E.-2: Holy O.N.E.s Meeting in Eternity

CHAPTER 19

Submission Versus Surrender

In the beginning, mankind was connected to the F.A.T.H.E.R. through a beam of light so glorious and powerful that it resonated in every living thing, in every moment. After mankind chose to go his own way, to be the combination of light and dark that comes with knowledge of *all* ways, the F.A.T.H.E.R.'s light was directed into the hearts and minds of those willing **S.O.U.L.S.** who sought after H.I.M.

S.O.U.L.S.: Spirits Outside of U.N.I.T.Y.'s Light Source

Those who looked for another path, apart from His presence (prescience) were not completely without His light, but they walked in darkness. In T.I.M.E., their darkness became a prison from which they could barely see the light. A prison of limitation that they could only be set free from by seeking H.I.M. with their whole H.E.A.R.T.

In today's world, many are in total darkness, and the light of L.I.F.E. has diminished in those who have chosen E.V.I.L. over G.O.O.D. When a person consciously chooses to be L.O.V.E., the Truth (W.A.Y.) is enhanced by the light of the F.A.T.H.E.R. through the pleading of the S.O.N.

Without the S.O.N. to intervene, the F.A.T.H.E.R. does not interfere. His W.I.L.L. for man is not in question—it is His W.I.L.L. that *mankind* triumph. But not all men will be part of that triumph, unless they **S.U.B.M.I.T.** to H.I.M.

S.U.B.M.I.T: S.U.R.R.E.N.D.E.R. Until Benevolence is Magnified and Interred in Truth

---

The process of becoming L.O.V.E. requires a willingness to S.U.B.M.I.T. in every moment. That means as the tendency to "go your own way" emerges in your life (and it will again and again), you must be *willing* (strong willed *in submission*) to His instruction. Without submission, the process of becoming L.O.V.E. is filled with transgression. It is not enough to simply "surrender" and then go about your business on your usual path. If you do this, expecting intervention without participation on your part, then you will find that you are technically "saved" but spiritually bereft.

Those without this insight are not B.E.I.N.G. L.O.V.E. in every moment. They are blind to the light of God's L.O.V.E. in their lives. Your eyes must be opened to the reality of the power of God's presence, just as you are being opened to the salvation offered through Jesus Christ. When you are B.E.I.N.G. L.O.V.E. your entire being (body, mind, spirit, heart) is aware of the changes occurring on a daily basis. But this level of awareness does not happen without *submission to the process.*

The Father's instruction comes in every moment of your life, and to simply turn away from it is the equivalent of denying His influence over your life. Your progress will be halted, even if your salvation is assured. Which type of servant do you wish to be? One who is in a partnership with your L.O.R.D. and S.A.V.I.O.R.? Or someone who is being changed without receiving any information about *how*, *why*, or *what* is happening?

Those who seek H.I.M. with *all* their H.E.A.R.T. know how His presence affects their journey. Those who ask for His guidance and listen for His instruction learn how to be L.O.V.E. in a way that benefits others around them.

When these children come to the Father for "forgiveness," to be restored from things in the world that have harmed them in some way, the Father sees them as He sees His own S.O.N.—worthy of redemption and G.R.A.C.E. because they are voluntarily submitting to His guidance. Submission is an ongoing requirement for those seeking to understand His intention for them and for those seeking a place of honor in His K.I.N.G.D.O.M.

Let me be clear, this is not about rewards, or even about mansions of glory, although those are used as metaphors to describe the places reserved for the pure of H.E.A.R.T. The real "reward" is recognition by the Father through the S.O.N. Just as He asks to be acknowledged by His children, He wants to know each one personally. This is only possible through the development of an intimate relationship with H.I.M. Submission is what is required to have that kind of relationship. He waits to impart His L.O.V.E. to you in every possible way—not in just an energetic way. He waits to *be your partner in L.O.V.E.*

Will you come to the **T.H.R.O.N.E.** with this kind of intimacy? Or will you arrive without the discovery of the depths of His L.O.V.E.? He wants to know you personally.

T.H.R.O.N.E.: Trinity's H.O.L.Y. Resonance at Origin/O.N.E.[1]

Christ says...

I Am the bridge. Cross over and learn of His undying affection for you personally. For each one is unique and special, and so is His Presence in your L.I.F.E. There is a path only you can walk and a song only you can sing. Submit to the joys of the journey and learn your song. It's the key to understanding your unique purpose and place in the Father's K.I.N.G.D.O.M."

---

[1] This specific reference to oneness within the acronym "T.H.R.O.N.E." distinctly refers to the energy of the Trinity (Father, Son and Holy Spirit) combined as one Omnipotent Neutral Energy, rather than the Omnipresent Neutral Energy previously described as part of Becoming L.O.V.E.

Chapter 19: Submission Versus Surrender

F.A.T.H.E.R.: Forever Abiding in the Truth of Heaven's Eternal Resonance/Residence
S.O.U.L.S.: Spirits Outside of U.N.I.T.Y.'s Light Source
H.I.M.: Holy Immanuel Manifested
U.N.I.T.Y.: Undying Neutral and Infinite Truth in Yahweh/You
T.I.M.E.: Temporal Insights Meted in Eternity
H.E.A.R.T.: Heaven's Eternal Alliance Resonating Truth
L.I.F.E.: Light Inside the Fabric of Eternity
E.V.I.L.: Energetic Vibrations Inverting L.I.F.E.
G.O.O.D.: God's Omnipresent, Omnipotent Domain
W.A.Y.: Wavelength Abiding in Yahweh/You
S.O.N.: Spirit Offered in Neutrality
W.I.L.L.: Word and Intention in L.I.F.E. and L.O.V.E
L.O.V.E.: Light Over Vibrational Energy
S.U.B.M.I.T.: S.U.R.R.E.N.D.E.R. Until Benevolence is Magnified and Interred in Truth
S.U.R.R.E.N.D.E.R.: Salvation Under a Relationship Resonating Eternally in the Neutral Domain of Everlasting Reciprocity
B.E.I.N.G.: Benevolent Entity Interred in Neutral G.O.O.D.
L.O.R.D.: L.O.V.E. Overtaking Rebellious Domains

S.A.V.I.O.R.: Spirit Abiding Vibrational Incarnation to Overcome Rebellion

H.E.A.R.T.: Heaven's Eternal Alliance Resonating Truth

G.R.A.C.E.: God's Resonating Alliance in C.H.R.I.S.T Eternal

C.H.R.I.S.T.: Consecrated, Holy, Resonating and Indwelling Spirit of Truth

K.I.N.G.D.O.M.: Kinetic Integration into Neutral G.O.O.D./God's Design of Omnipotent Manifestation

T.H.R.O.N.E.: Trinity's H.O.L.Y., Resonance at Origin/O.N.E. (Omnipotent Neutral Energy)

O.N.E.: Omnipresent, Neutral, Eternal

H.O.L.Y.: Heaven's Omnipotent Light in Yahweh/You

CHAPTER 20

Revival

Your course correction comes from your own desire to be near The F.A.T.H.E.R. His W.I.L.L. was implanted in your B.E.I.N.G. long before it was subjected to the counter-vibrational forces of E.V.I.L. In that sense, you are uncorruptible. However, your actions bring consequences, and until you *choose* The F.A.T.H.E.R. over all else, your mind is subject to transgression in the world. By that I mean, wandering from the Truth (W.A.Y.) that will lead you to your **N.E.W. H.O.M.E.**

**N.E.W. H.O.M.E.: Neutral Energetic W.A.Y.
for Holy Ones Meeting in Eternity**

The universe is a single mind that is divided into two parts—just as your own mind is divided--wavelengths of light and densities made from *part light* and *part dark matter*. The dark matter of the universe serves its own purpose, while the **L.I.G.H.T.** serves the W.I.L.L. of The F.A.T.H.E.R.

**L.I.G.H.T.: L.O.V.E.'s Infinite
Guardian of His Truth**

Darkness serves to make B.E.I.N.G.S. in matter subject to its densities so that matter is attached to them and to their environment. It presides over people in the same way—to subject each person to a limited experience, defined by density and ruled by thought *alone*.

But, The F.A.T.H.E.R.'S K.I.N.G.D.O.M. is not bound by any limitation. His L.I.G.H.T. is able to go anywhere, through time and space, and to traverse the limits of the universe without impediment. His L.I.G.H.T. can be/come whenever and wherever it is sent. This allows for acts of creation throughout *all* of creation. It is His L.I.G.H.T. that sparks the flame of creation. When the world fell from alignment to His L.I.G.H.T. alone, it was captured by a series of wavelengths that are attached to dark matter. Density was increased, as was density of thought (mind). When the mind is captured in this way, its tendencies are to rely on what it can see, touch and feel, to know (think).

In the F.A.T.H.E.R.'S K.I.N.G.D.O.M. knowing is simply B.E.I.N.G. (not thinking) and experience does not require thought first to understand—thought is part of experience, as it happens, not before. In the W.O.R.L.D., experience is only realized (known, but not necessarily understood) *after* the encounter. In all of creation, this is a condition that remains tentative and dependent upon the choices each makes. The world was His creation for re-creation. The world is actually the center of the battleground for all of creation for one simple reason—the choice made here is the choice made for all. This is why those human beings talking to "guides" are being told of things to come and ways to enhance their experience through the prism of "love". But, these "guides" do not understand that their interference in the direct guidance provided by The F.A.T.H.E.R. is actually confusing those on earth, and thereby delaying their process to the degree that when The F.A.T.H.E.R. shakes the heavens and the earth into a N.E.W. creation, those remaining outside of His protection will not be A.B.L.E. to become a part of it.

This is why it is imperative that all human beings T.R.U.S.T. in J.E.S.U.S. at this time. It is only a matter of time (and matter in time) before the N.E.W. vibrational frequencies will arrive here. And, when His W.I.L.L. arrives, the condition of the world and everything in it will be forever changed. He wants His people to survive it and to thrive in the new creation, which will be without (void of all) darkness. His L.I.G.H.T. alone will be. Those residing (re-siding) in His L.I.G.H.T. through the transformation provided by His S.O.N. will be A.B.L.E. to withstand the transformation of the world, as well as His arrival.

When you *think*, you open your mind to the counter-vibrational wavelengths designed to attach you to the current condition of the world. When you are B.E.I.N.G. L.O.V.E. you are rising above those vibrations in a way that prevents attachment. Your actions (thoughts and engagements) while in the world require continual cleansing (redemption and renewal) daily.

Christ says...

"I Am the way to bathe in the L.I.G.H.T. I Am the L.I.G.H.T. that is sent to cleanse those waiting for admission to His K.I.N.G.D.O.M. It is that simple. I Am your redeemer for renewal of your body and spirit, that you would be transformed in the same way that I was transformed in death. However, the time is coming when you need not D.I.E. in the process of transformation. I Am

here to bring you H.O.M.E.[1] But you must come willingly (by your own submission) for I do not work with (or in) an unwilling heart. Your counter-vibrational center is in your mind, my L.I.G.H.T. resides in willing hearts, and eventually consumes the mind, thereby changing it from divided (both higher and lower frequencies) into a mind unified by His L.I.G.H.T. You will still have thoughts of negativity and experiences of it, because you are in the W.O.R.L.D.; and, others in your life and their experiences will generate those thoughts around you. Your job is to avoid taking them into your B.E.I.N.G. I Am your shield of protection. When I reside in each of you and you willingly declare that I will be your redeemer, I Am A.B.L.E. to wipe away these "stains" of transgression. I recommend coming to me daily, to prevent the build-up of those wavelengths that cause pain and death, for they are the source of disease (dis-ease) in your body and mind. Come to me for P.E.A.C.E. of mind and body, and I Am will give you R.E.S.T.

Re-membering is the key to revival. Your free will allows for the choice—to become L.O.V.E. or to remain in darkness. The choice is yours; however, the experience provided for those who come freely to His L.I.G.H.T. is nothing like the experience waiting for those who wish to remain in darkness. He has already willed the L.I.G.H.T. of eternity for those who choose H.I.M. It is a forgone conclusion that must be brought to fruition. His W.I.L.L. is the defining element. Do not mistake your freedom in this equation apart from His dominion over all things. I Am telling you this for one reason—**A.L.L. I.S. O.N.E.**

---

[1] Christ's reference to H.O.M.E. here is intended to encompass both meanings: the process of transformation -Holy Ones Manifesting in Emeth/Eternity and also the result of transformation- Holy Ones Meeting in Eternity.

A.L.L. I.S. O.N.E.: Alpha's Love Light of Immanent Space/Spirit is Omnipotent, Neutral and Eternal

In the end, all will become one mind, one heart, one experience. Those outside of My protection will not enter the experience designed for every-thing, because nothing else will exist. Time is coming to a rapid conclusion. **R.E.V.I.V.A.L.** *must begin in each of you, with you, by you,* **before** *His arrival."*

R.E.V.I.V.A.L.: Resonate Eternity's Vitro Inside Vivo[2] & Amidst L.O.V.E.

I Am coming soon to take those who are already with (in) M.E. to the place prepared for them, while those who wish to remain in darkness are given the full experience of it. Come to the T.H.R.O.N.E. cleansed of the wavelengths that bind you here. Come to M.E. for renewal, P.E.A.C.E. and R.E.S.T."

---

[2] This combined use of both in Vitro (in a test tube) while inside Vivo (in the living) is a reference to the transformation of Humanity while separated from all that I.S. It is also a description of "investigating something within its living context that has been taken out of its context". *See Quora.com, Brian Farley, Molecular and Cell Biology Postdoc, UC Berkley 4-22-15 for additional information on Vitro in Vivo.*

Chapter 20: Revival

F.A.T.H.E.R.: Forever Abiding in the Truth of Heaven's Eternal Resonance/Residence

W.I.L.L.: Word and Intention in L.I.F.E. and L.O.V.E

L.I.F.E.: Light Inside the Fabric of Eternity

L.O.V.E.: Light Over Vibrational Energy

B.E.I.N.G.: Benevolent Entity Interred in Neutral G.O.O.D.

G.O.O.D.: God's Omnipresent, Omnipotent Domain

E.V.I.L.: Energetic Vibrations Inverting L.I.F.E.

W.A.Y.: Wavelength Abiding in Yahweh/You

N.E.W. H.O.M.E.: Neutral Energetic W.A.Y. for Holy Ones Meeting in Eternity

L.I.G.H.T.: L.O.V.E.'s Infinite Guardian of His Truth

K.I.N.G.D.O.M.: Kinetic Integration into Neutral G.O.O.D./God's Design of Omnipotent Manifestation

W.O.R.L.D.: War Of Rebellion in L.O.V.E.'s Domain

N.E.W.: Neutral, Eternal W.A.Y.

A.B.L.E.: Abiding in the Benevolent Light of Eternity

T.R.U.S.T.: Truth Resonating in U.N.I.T.Y. with the S.O.N. in T.I.M.E

U.N.I.T.Y.: Undying Neutral and Infinite Truth in Yahweh/You

S.O.N.: Spirit Offered in Neutrality

T.I.M.E.: Temporal Insights Meted in Eternity

J.E.S.U.S.: Jehovah's Eternal Spirit Under/Unified in the S.O.N.

D.I.E.: Disintegrate Internally and Eternally

H.O.M.E.: Holy O.N.E.s Manifesting in Emeth/Eternity

P.E.A.C.E.: Predominating Energy with Acceptance of C.H.R.I.S.T. Eternally

C.H.R.I.S.T.: Consecrated, Holy, Resonating and Indwelling Spirit of Truth

R.E.S.T.: Resonate Energetically in the Sanctity of Truth

H.I.M.: Holy Immanuel Manifested

A.L.L. I.S. O.N.E.: Alpha's Love Light of Immanent Space/Spirit is Omnipotent, Neutral and Eternal

R.E.V.I.V.A.L.: Resonate Eternity's Vitro Inside Vivo & Amidst L.O.V.E.

M.E.: Manifest Eternity

T.H.R.O.N.E.: Trinity's H.O.L.Y. Resonance at Origin/O.N.E.

H.O.L.Y.: Heaven's Omnipotent Light in Yahweh/You

O.N.E.: Omnipresent, Neutral, Eternal

CHAPTER 21

The River of Life

Christ says...

*"P.R.A.Y.E.R. is the answer to everything. Many people see it as a means to an end, but the Truth (W.A.Y.) for anything to be made real is through the collaborative nature and power of P.R.A.Y.E.R. Mankind was given a special relationship with The F.A.T.H.E.R. for the purpose of co-creating in the physical realms of the creation. By physical, I mean those dimensions of existence that support lower vibrational creations. Trees, rocks, earth, sky—are all manifested by The F.A.T.H.E.R. and managed by mankind. It's is no secret that "management" is being questioned. But more importantly, **why** is there no agreement on how and what to do and to say to one another about the condition of the world, and all of the people in it? Everyone recognizes turmoil and strife, but the collective consciousness to enact any solution lacks the willpower to manage change, even a conscious change.*

*So, there is a "pickle" in the process—even those who S.E.E. cannot effect change without those who are **B.L.I.N.D.E.D**.*

B.L.I.N.D.E.D.: Beyond L.O.V.E.'s Influence and in Nature's Dominion of Energetic Dissonance

It is M.Y. presence that empowers those who can S.E.E. to enact what must be accomplished. I Am A.B.L.E. to empower them through redemption (unity of heart, body, spirit and mind). But it is The F.A.T.H.E.R. who provides the power of His W.I.L.L. in the reformed human being that is A.B.L.E. to overcome dissention and division. His W.I.L.L. power is stronger than any collective will of man. So, you only S.E.E. with eyes of limitation, and your ability to affect the type of change that brings renewal is dependent upon two things: redemption of heart and mind through The S.O.N., and enablement (in-A.B.L.E.-ment) through The F.A.T.H.E.R.

How does someone who is B.L.I.N.D.E.D. begin this process? By praying for Me to enter your H.E.A.R.T. and change it. How does anyone proceed through the process of redemption (transformation)? By praying in My N.A.M.E.[1] to The F.A.T.H.E.R. for guidance and then listening for His instruction. He delivers results to those who K.N.O.W. M.Y. voice, and who come willingly to follow His **W.O.R.D.***s.*

---

[1] Here "name" is also referring to the audible words "Jesus Christ" as the name above all names and the One given power and authority by The Father to intercede on our behalf. It is important to also note that the spoken name of Jesus (not just the concept of a Neutral Amalgam in Manifest Eternity) carries with it a very powerful energetic signature as He is the person who became the Spirit of Truth for all.

W.O.R.D.: Wavelengths of Omnipotent Resonance and Dominion

*How does anyone come to understand the journey? Through trial and tribulation that prepares the person's B.E.I.N.G. at every level of existence. Prayer for understanding and enlightenment (being in the L.I.G.H.T.) comes as part of the epiphanies revealed along The W.A.Y. Prayer for His W.I.L.L. to be done and not your own, is key to the successful transformation of your own B.E.I.N.G., but also to the successful transfer of the power of His W.I.L.L. You must freely give up your sense of self-control and willingly enter the **S.T.R.E.A.M.** of L.I.F.E. that only He provides.*

S.T.R.E.A.M.: Sanctified in Truth and Resonating Eternity's Alliance with Manifestation

*Once fully immersed in the S.T.R.E.A.M. of L.I.F.E. it becomes a **R.I.V.E.R.** of L.I.F.E. for those manifesting change through the empowerment of their own S.O.U.L.s.*

R.I.V.E.R.: Resonance Interred in Victory's Eternal Residence

"The S.O.U.L. is trapped in a "body" of limitation, but the entire process is designed to bring you to a point of no return—a point of acceptance of His W.I.L.L. over your

own, and the ability to co-create once again, with The F.A.T.H.E.R.'s H.A.N.D. reaching down to guide you at every step. Once a H.U.M.A.N. B.E.I.N.G. has reached this point, He/She is beyond the reaches of the E.N.E.M.Y. within. And, for those not yet at this point of no return, the triumphant B.E.I.N.G. must P.R.A.Y. for O.T.H.E.R.s to accept His W.I.L.L. in order for the progress that must be realized to be made manifest for A.L.L. The power of the P.R.A.Y.E.R.s of those who are in the R.I.V.E.R. of L.I.F.E. are given high priority, and are accompanied by a type of "super charge" that comes from, and returns to The F.A.T.H.E.R. (source) with an intensity and speed that is unmatched in all of creation. **_So the speeding up of T.I.M.E. and of change is actually accomplished by those in the R.I.V.E.R. of L.I.F.E._** *It is relative to the engagement of those who are B.E.I.N.G. L.O.V.E. for all of those who are not yet becoming L.O.V.E. This is why mankind must P.R.A.Y. for more people to engage with M.E. (The S.O.N.) and to receive the blessings offered through M.E. for the transformation of their B.E.I.N.G. and their W.O.R.L.D. The two are not separate processes but trying to achieve O.N.E. without the O.T.H.E.R., is not a sustainable effort. In point of fact, it is a futile endeavor. For those who prefer to believe (be the lie) of separation and self-sufficiency, their way will only produce halting and ultimately, temporary results. But the Truth (the sure W.A.Y.) produces a lasting and permanent victory over darkness for A.L.L. and is not just a personal victory. And the route to that victory begins and ends with P.R.A.Y.E.R.*

Ask M.E. to enter your H.E.A.R.T. today. If you have not done this already, I Am waiting for you to decide (de-side) and join the only army dedicated to the U.N.I.T.Y. of A.L.L. that I.S. and the reformation of the whole

(H.O.L.Y.) creation. Become L.O.V.E. now, and begin with this simple prayer:

> "Lord Jesus, I am ready to accept the power of your presence in my L.I.F.E. Come into my H.E.A.R.T. and redeem it. Work with me to establish understanding of His W.A.Y.s. Guide and instruct me for the benefit of my own S.O.U.L. and for the benefit of A.L.L. that I.S. I am waiting to receive Y.O.U., with all of my heart, and I give it freely, in S.U.R.R.E.N.D.E.R. of my own will. Come Lord Jesus, come."

Will you lay down your burdens and pick up mine? Will you dedicate your H.E.A.R.T., M.I.N.D. and spirit for the salvation of A.L.L. that I.S.? Are you wishing for a lasting P.E.A.C.E. of heart and mind? Then ask for it. And then remember to ask for all that follows in M.Y. N.A.M.E. For the R.I.V.E.R. of L.I.F.E. awaits those who seek it, and The F.A.T.H.E.R. waits for those He has called to respond to His calling.

Chapter 21: The River of Life

P.R.A.Y.E.R.: Protected/Personal Resonance Aligned with Yahweh's Eternal Resonance
W.A.Y.: Wavelength Abiding in Yahweh/You
F.A.T.H.E.R.: Forever Abiding in the Truth of Heaven's Eternal Resonance/Residence
S.E.E.: Seek, Experience, Enlighten
B.L.I.N.D.E.D.: Beyond L.O.V.E.'s Influence and in Nature's Dominion of Energetic Dissonance
L.O.V.E.: Light Over Vibrational Energy
M.Y.: Manifest Yahweh
I A.M.: Infinite Almighty Manifestation
A.B.L.E.: Abiding in the Benevolent Light of Eternity
W.I.L.L.: Word and Intention in L.I.F.E. and L.O.V.E
L.I.F.E.: Light Inside the Fabric of Eternity
S.O.N.: Spirit Offered in Neutrality
H.E.A.R.T.: Heaven's Eternal Alliance Resonating Truth
N.A.M.E.: Neutral Amalgam in Manifest Eternity
K.N.O.W.: Know No O.T.H.E.R. Way/Wavelength
O.T.H.E.R.: Omnipresent Transmissions Heating/Hating Emmanuel's Resonance
W.O.R.D.: Wavelengths of Omnipotent Resonance and Dominion
B.E.I.N.G.: Benevolent Entity Interred in Neutral G.O.O.D.
G.O.O.D.: God's Omnipresent, Omnipotent Domain

S.T.R.E.A.M.: Sanctified in Truth and Resonating Eternity's Alliance with Manifestation

R.I.V.E.R.: Resonance Interred in Victory's Eternal Residence

S.O.U.L.S.: Spirits Outside of U.N.I.T.Y.'s Light Source

H.A.N.D.: Heaven's Alliance in Neutral Dominion

H.U.M.A.N.: His Ultimate Manifestation Abiding in Neutrality

E.N.E.M.Y.: Energetic Network of E.V.I.L. Magnetized/Magnified in You

E.V.I.L.: Energetic Vibrations Inverting L.I.F.E.

A.L.L.: Alpha's L.O.V.E. Light

T.I.M.E.: Temporal Insights Meted in Eternity

M.E.: Manifest Eternity

W.O.R.L.D.: War Of Rebellion in L.O.V.E.'s Domain

O.N.E.: Omnipresent, Neutral, Eternal

U.N.I.T.Y.: Undying Neutral and Infinite Truth in Yahweh/You

I.S.: Immanent Source/Spirit/Space

H.O.L.Y.: Heaven's Omnipotent Light in Yahweh/You

Y.O.U.: Yahweh's Omnipresent U.N.I.T.Y.

S.U.R.R.E.N.D.E.R.: Salvation Under a Relationship Resonating Eternally in the Neutral Domain of Everlasting Reciprocity

M.I.N.D.: Manifest Intention from Neutral Dominion

P.E.A.C.E.: Predominating Energy with Acceptance of C.H.R.I.S.T. Eternally

C.H.R.I.S.T.: Consecrated, Holy, Resonating and Indwelling Spirit of Truth

CHAPTER 22
Straying

Christ says...

Look to the heavens for I Am waiting to bring you H.O.M.E. I Am able to undo the daily transgressions that assault your B.E.I.N.G. I came for this purpose—and I died to be your bridge to eternity. Each person makes mistakes daily. There is no perfect human, one who is more A.B.L.E. than I to deliver you from the stains of the world. That is why it is important to understand that His O.N.L.Y. S.O.N. can remove the sins (things that separate) you from The Father. You can never be separated from His L.O.V.E., for He has designed you with a heart that carries H.I.M. in it. However, your own will can be in opposition to His W.I.L.L. for you because you have been given the choice— to come H.O.M.E. or to go your own way.

*The parable of the L.O.S.T. Son tells of the prodigal son, the one who strayed away and ultimately returned to his father when his resources ran out. He "spent" himself in the world, only to find hunger and destitution and loneliness. Luckily, he had a father who loved him beyond his actions and forgave him of all his transgressions. For his father cared only that his child was returned without harm, and not for what had transpired in his absence. **It is the same with your Father.** He sent Me to bear the burden for all* men so that you too can return H.O.M.E. without blame or consequence.

It is only in L.O.V.E. that He sends Me, and not as an agent of wrath or judgment. I Am not a choice, an idea, or a belief. I Am the W.A.Y., the Truth, and the L.I.F.E. And no man comes to the Father but by M.E.[1] I Am A.B.L.E. because I was cleansed of the world's transgression on the cross and born into the world through the F.A.T.H.E.R.'s seed. In both instances, I Am unattached to the worldly vibration that connects you to the conditions here. I Am free of those attachments and My life was modeled in such a way to help M.E. understand **your** struggle from **your** perspective. I Am A.B.L.E. because I have the experience of your burden and I overcame it by the power of The Father's L.O.V.E. The same is offered to you, and you only need to accept this gift that is freely given.

It is not a burden for Me now; it is an honor to bring H.O.M.E. those who choose The Father's L.O.V.E. over their own will. Those who believe that I Am A.B.L.E. find a peace that "surpasses understanding." It is a leap of F.A.I.T.H. for those who choose Me, because the W.A.Y. is not revealed **until the choice is made.**

I beseech those of you who are "thinking" about it to consider this: What if The Father, the Supreme Being, the Creator of All (whatever name you call Him by) meant for you to find Him through a lifetime of trial and, ultimately, tribulation for one reason? What if that reason is that He is the O.N.L.Y. God in whom you can T.R.U.S.T., and to find the W.A.Y. you had to learn of false gods before finding H.I.M.?

---

[1] Jesus is referring to scripture here, specifically John 14:6

In your present condition, the only means to know something for certain is to become certain by way of trial and error. The only way to become the L.I.G.H.T. is to be enlightened. Who does the lighting up? Do you believe that you are the source of all creation? Do you believe that you are able to generate, on your own, the power of transformation? Do you think (decide) for yourself which paths to take on your life's journey? Or are they often presented to you as opportunities that you choose to engage with along the way? What brought you to today? Was it a belief that you are the architect of your own life with the forethought and the power to send you where you would go? Or have you relied on guidance, intuition, synchronicity, and the kindness of others? What brought you to these pages?

If your answer is that you were guided in some way, or that synchronicities occurred that opened a series of events prior to your arrival here, then I suggest that you pray for clarity about the reason you are reading this now, and not sooner or later. I Am B.E.I.N.G. L.O.V.E. for all who seek eternal life, but I Am only A.B.L.E. to bring those who acknowledge M.E. as their S.A.V.I.O.R. (the O.N.E. who is A.B.L.E. to deliver The Father's L.I.G.H.T.). Those who are seeking to be "enlightened" by any other source than The S.O.U.R.C.E. are being misled. Those who appear to generate "light that sparkles" and come in the form of "light orbs" are generating a false light for the purpose of drawing you closer (pulling you in) to their network. There are two networks—opposing forces that pull in different directions. The powers of darkness often interfere with the True process of enlightenment (Becoming L.O.V.E.) by presenting themselves as "enlightened" guides. If you consider yourself a "child of the light," consider this: It is possible to be in a light that is not The L.I.G.H.T.

If you could see into the darkness, you could discern the Truth on your own. But your human condition prevents insight of this kind because darkness is also present in you, and not solely outside of your B.E.I.N.G. I Am pure L.I.G.H.T., and The Father has anointed Me to replace darkness in you with His L.I.G.H.T. Those of you who have been given abilities to see and hear people who have passed into another realm are most susceptible to misleading because often you have come to believe in your own gift more than you believe in Me. If this is you, then your gift has become an idol (distraction) that you worship (rely on).

If you have these kinds of gifts, you have them for a reason. If you have been given sight, it is not because you have insight into God's W.I.L.L. but rather as a lesson for your S.O.U.L.'s benefit. The lesson is this: to come to the point where you understand that His W.I.L.L. alone (and not your own) can bring you out of darkness. His children are subjected to this test throughout their lives because they have asked that Truth be revealed to them in a way that is certain. And this test often comes with extra-sensory-perception. But this ability is not truth (proof)—it's a distraction designed to magnify the Truth. The W.A.Y. is only certain when F.A.I.T.H. is your sight—not "seeing" the dead or talking with spirits or "learning" that which is imparted from beings claiming to reside beyond this realm. In fact, the kind of "learning" I Am referring to is the most dangerous form of teaching for those on the "spiritual" path. For without My presence in your heart and mind, you are susceptible to great misleading.

I Am the only Truth (W.A.Y.) to The Father's L.I.G.H.T.; all others claiming to possess personal power to heal you or to transform you are false gods, false prophets, and false teachers. Do not mistake their information (or anything) from beyond this realm for Truth (the W.A.Y.) that will lead you out of darkness. Most "guides" do not even attempt to claim that they can deliver you, for they understand that they do not possess this ability. What they confuse for an advanced state of being is actually a lower level of existence to your own. Their experience is unlike that of mankind. To try to tell you how to transcend without knowledge of how they themselves are transcending (even if well intended) is damaging to you. Do not listen to those who promise "peace" and "light" and "love" in the form of rituals or rocks or anything from the natural or supernatural world, for they are being misled themselves. And if you are talking to D.E.M.O.N.S., which you may not realize, then know this: They have one purpose and one only: **to use your light to power their own source of being.**

The fallen are lower forms of beings that have become "vampires of light," and they are in the world to trap mankind into belief (an energetic connection) in their power. In actuality, they have no power. They use your power for their purposes. And they use your light to cover their true appearance. They are D.E.M.O.N.S. of darkness hiding in your light.

Do not attempt to work with them, for the only result will be your eternal dissent into darkness. Once your light is consumed by their darkness, whether by disease of body or of mind, your chances of bringing yourself back to God's/G.O.O.D.'s L.I.G.H.T. through any worldly technology or treatment is less than zero. I Am the cure for depression, disease, heartache, separation and loneliness, and I Am the only O.N.E. who can bring you into the everlasting light of The Father's K.I.N.G.D.O.M. There is only O.N.E. eternal L.I.G.H.T. and only one lamp with this eternal flame. Come back to the Father who loves you without question and waits to celebrate your return. Come home by W.A.Y. of the Truth (sure path) and live (deny death by darkness).

Chapter 22: Straying

H.O.M.E.: Holy O.N.E.s Manifesting in Emeth/Eternity

O.N.E.: Omnipresent, Neutral, Eternal

B.E.I.N.G.: Benevolent Entity Interred in Neutral G.O.O.D.

G.O.O.D.: God's Omnipresent, Omnipotent Domain

A.B.L.E.: Abiding in the Benevolent Light of Eternity

O.N.L.Y. S.O.N.: Omnipresent Neutral Light of Yahweh's Spirit Offered in Neutrality

L.O.V.E.: Light Over Vibrational Energy

H.I.M.: Holy Immanuel Manifested

W.I.L.L.: Word and Intention in L.I.F.E. and L.O.V.E

L.I.F.E.: Light Inside the Fabric of Eternity

L.O.S.T.: Living Outside of the Spirit of Truth

W.A.Y.: Wavelength Abiding in Yahweh/You

M.E.: Manifest Eternity

F.A.T.H.E.R.: Forever Abiding in the Truth of Heaven's Eternal Resonance/Residence

F.A.I.T.H.: Forever Accepting the Interred Truth in Him

O.N.L.Y.: Omnipresent Neutral Light in Yahweh/You

T.R.U.S.T.: Truth Resonating in U.N.I.T.Y. with the S.O.N. in T.I.M.E

U.N.I.T.Y.: Undying Neutral and Infinite Truth in Yahweh/You

S.O.N.: Spirit Offered in Neutrality

T.I.M.E.: Temporal Insights Meted in Eternity

L.I.G.H.T.: L.O.V.E.'s Infinite Guardian of His Truth

S.A.V.I.O.R.: Spirit Abiding Vibrational Incarnation to Overcome Rebellion

O.N.E.: Omnipresent, Neutral, Eternal

S.O.U.R.C.E.: Sanctified Omnipotent U.N.I.T.Y. Resonating in C.H.R.I.S.T. Eternally

C.H.R.I.S.T.: Consecrated, Holy, Resonating and Indwelling Spirit of Truth

S.O.U.L.S.: Spirits Outside of U.N.I.T.Y.'s Light Source

D.E.M.O.N.S.: Destructive Energies/Entities Manifesting in Omnipresent Neutral Spirit

CHAPTER 23

Cooperation

The way to heaven is blocked by a series of vibrations designed to hold you in bondage to the world. When I say "world," I mean your experience as you now know it to be. **The truth is that the experience of the world has been corrupted, and the true experience hidden from view.** In the beginning, there was no counter-vibration capable of entering your mind and convincing you of any other thing, because your mind was not susceptible to such thought. It was not divided unto itself. Deception was necessary to lead you astray and to open the door of **D.O.U.B.T.**

D.O.U.B.T.: D.E.N.I.A.L. Obscuring Unrestricted B.E.I.N.G.s in Truth

---

Your condition is primarily a case of internal strife-*with yourself.* Am I able? Can I do this alone? What are my options? Where do I go for help? How do I become a better, happier, more fulfilled person? You once knew the answers to these questions because you were once whole and at O.N.E. with The F.A.T.H.E.R. But since the divisions took hold (separation from H.I.M., division between heart and mind, and division within your mind) you have been convinced of the permanence of separation and the untrue experience of isolation.

Christ says...

*"When I came into the world, I came to redeem it, and you/**Y.O.U.***

Y.O.U.: Yahweh's Omnipresent U.N.I.T.Y.

---

*Redemption of B.E.I.N.G.s who have been given free will is a long and painstaking process, because their freedom to choose their own path is a sacred and honored state. However, in your case, The Father did not intend to allow the **E.N.E.M.Y.** the right to control your thoughts.*

E.N.E.M.Y.: Energetic Network of E.V.I.L. Magnetized/Magnified in You

---

So, the need for a redeemer is more vital for mankind than for any other creation—because the E.N.E.M.Y. came here to "own" you in ways that are not lawful (right). The true test of belief in Me is one of complete S.U.R.R.E.N.D.E.R. for this reason. You cannot determine the Truth (W.A.Y.) on your own because your body and mind are subjected to relentless assaults of counter-vibrational origin. They are lies that corrupt your mind in ways that lead to hopelessness, despair, and ultimately D.E.A.T.H. in the sense that you stop seeking the Father through M.E. Without M.E. there is no redemption for S.O.U.L.S. in peril. There is only O.N.E. W.A.Y. H.O.M.E.—and I Am the appointed messenger, priest, healer, and redeemer of men's S.O.U.L.s.

Your job is simply to cooperate. By this, I mean to be cooperative in the process designed to help you to overcome each and every stain, each and every "chord" (wavelength) that binds you to a false experience here and separates you from the Truth of who you really are and from The Father. Those who cooperate will find a symbiotic relationship of co-operation awaits them. For only together, through a series of realizations about what is G.O.O.D. (an extension of God) and what is righteous (correct) and what is Truth (Emeth, the sure path), are you able to overcome the condition of the W.O.R.L.D. **He waits to renew the Earth, because He waits for you to be ready to survive it.** *In our dance of cooperation, you will be asked to:*

- *Come to Me and ask for healing*
- *Open your heart to M.E. to receive My presence*
- *Open your mind and S.U.R.R.E.N.D.E.R. your own thoughts (will)*
- *P.R.A.Y. daily for deliverance from E.V.I.L.*
- *Experience the Truth (W.A.Y.) and learn from it*
- *Realize that I Am renewing your H.E.A.R.T., body, mind and spirit*
- *Admit your inability to do this on your own*
- *T.R.U.S.T. that I Am making you whole (H.O.L.Y.)*
- *Invite M.E. into every aspect of your L.I.F.E., every day in P.R.A.Y.E.R.*
- *Omit the things from your L.I.F.E. that bind you to the W.O.R.L.D.*
- *K.N.E.E.L. before The F.A.T.H.E.R. and ask to be taken H.O.M.E.*

K.N.E.E.L.: K.N.O.W. and No Energy Except L.O.V.E.

There is nothing more for you to do. Your responsibility begins and ends with F.A.I.T.H.

*Your only task is to believe that I Am able to bring you H.O.M.E. to the F.A.T.H.E.R.'s K.I.N.G.D.O.M. and allow M.E. to work in you/Y.O.U. to accomplish it. Cooperation begins with trusting that I Am A.B.L.E. I have earned the right from The Father, and with His permission, I Am asking you to allow Me, of your own free will, to prove to you that I Am A.B.L.E. The E.N.E.M.Y. never asked you, nor did the E.N.E.M.Y. earn the right to take your being into its control mechanisms. You have been kidnapped. With your cooperation, **I A.M.** can set you free.*

I A.M.: Infinite Almighty Manifestation

Chapter 23: Cooperation

D.O.U.B.T.: D.E.N.I.A.L. Obscuring Unrestricted B.E.I.N.G.s in Truth

D.E.N.I.A.L.: Damaging Energies/Entities Negating Infinity's Alliance with L.O.V.E.

B.E.I.N.G.: Benevolent Entity Interred in Neutral G.O.O.D.

G.O.O.D.: God's Omnipresent, Omnipotent Domain

L.O.V.E.: Light Over Vibrational Energy

O.N.E.: Omnipresent, Neutral, Eternal

F.A.T.H.E.R.: Forever Abiding in the Truth of Heaven's Eternal Resonance/Residence

H.I.M.: Holy Immanuel Manifested

Y.O.U.: Yahweh's Omnipresent U.N.I.T.Y.

U.N.I.T.Y.: Undying Neutral and Infinite Truth in Yahweh/You

E.N.E.M.Y.: Energetic Network of E.V.I.L. Magnetized/Magnified in You

E.V.I.L.: Energetic Vibrations Inverting L.I.F.E.

L.I.F.E.: Light Inside the Fabric of Eternity

S.U.R.R.E.N.D.E.R.: Salvation Under a Relationship Resonating Eternally in the Neutral Domain of Everlasting Reciprocity

W.A.Y.: Wavelength Abiding in Yahweh/You

D.E.A.T.H.: Dissonant Energy Altered Through Heat/Hate

179

M.E.: Manifest Eternity

S.O.U.L.S.: Spirits Outside of U.N.I.T.Y.'s Light Source

H.O.M.E.: Holy O.N.E.s Manifesting in Emeth/Eternity

W.O.R.L.D.: War Of Rebellion in L.O.V.E.'s Domain

P.R.A.Y.E.R.: Protected/Personal Resonance Aligned with Yahweh's Eternal Resonance

H.E.A.R.T.: Heaven's Eternal Alliance Resonating Truth

T.R.U.S.T.: Truth Resonating in U.N.I.T.Y. with the S.O.N. in T.I.M.E

S.O.N.: Spirit Offered in Neutrality

T.I.M.E.: Temporal Insights Meted in Eternity

H.O.L.Y.: Heaven's Omnipotent Light in Yahwey/You

K.N.E.E.L.: K.N.O.W. and No Energy Except L.O.V.E.

K.N.O.W.: Know No O.T.H.E.R. Way/Wavelength

O.T.H.E.R.: Omnipresent Transmissions Heating/Hating Emmanuel's Resonance

F.A.I.T.H.: Forever Accepting the Interred Truth in Him

K.I.N.G.D.O.M.: Kinetic Integration into Neutral G.O.O.D./God's Design of Omnipotent Manifestation

A.B.L.E.: Abiding in the Benevolent Light of Eternity

I A.M.: Infinite Almighty Manifestation

CHAPTER 24

Loving

Christ says...
Loving is an act. It's not a thought nor is it an emotion. It's a state of being that requires relinquishment of one's own sense of well-being in a way that places the well-being of others first. When you are B.E.I.N.G. L.O.V.E., it is easy to see results through acts of love. Kindness, patience, forgiveness—these are all loving actions. Being kind to another person reaches them in ways that simply thinking about being kind could never accomplish. Being patient with a child, a troubled soul, or a person in addiction takes energy that many don't have to give. Despite good intentions and best wishes for their well-being, without loving acts to back up those intentions, the giver is bereft of the benefits of love and so is the intended recipient. Giving is at the heart of loving.

I Am A.B.L.E. to give those who seek Me the strength they need to love others as they love themselves. It is true that you must fill your own cup so that it runs over before you can be L.O.V.E. for another. I Am A.B.L.E. to provide all that is needed for a love-filled heart to be expressed in a loving life. Come to Me for "peace" and "rest" and you will also find increased capacity to "love" another person.

You may think that you are a great lover right now. But if you do not know Me, or My W.A.Y.s, you do not know My heart for humanity. It is beyond anything that mankind can feel for itself. Each of you is capable of loving those who love you back. That is easy. But I A.M. A.B.L.E. to L.O.V.E. even when you despise Me, when you ignore Me, when you turn away from Me. I A.M. A.B.L.E. to L.O.V.E. in all circumstances because I know who you really are and what is waiting to be revealed that is now deep inside each of you, trapped and undermined (under-mind) in ways that you cannot understand (stand under). The pressure to love in a world besieged by E.V.I.L. cannot be overcome without divine intervention.

I Am your counselor.

I Am your guide.

I A.M. A.B.L.E. to restore the world and your heart's innermost desire because I Am the author of the original floor plan.

The world has been remodeled since The Father willed it into being. But I A.M. also the architect of the remodel. And if you will cooperate, My W.A.Y. will bear the kind of fruit (results) in your heart that cannot be changed by the W.O.R.L.D. Despite the attempts of those around you to pull you into hatred and F.E.A.R., a heart that is committed to salvation through M.E. is a heart that comes with a warranty, a declaration of salvation freely given for all of eternity.

Do you believe that you are able to change your being into one that can withstand the trials and tribulations of the world? If you think so, then perhaps changes that are occurring throughout the world do not bother you. Are you at peace with the issues of human trafficking, slavery, starvation, and murder? Do you think that you can change others in ways that will eliminate these conditions permanently and restore peace for all? If you are a realist, then you must confess that you alone can accomplish very little. If you are a pragmatist, you must confess that society's best and brightest have come together many times but ultimately failed to create a lasting peace. When will you try **L.O.V.I.N.G.** *the world into a new state of B.E.I.N.G. instead of just thinking about it?*

L.O.V.I.N.G.: Light Overcoming Vibrations Invading/Inverting Neutral G.O.O.D.

Do you believe the "positive energies" sent out into the world by well-intended souls are enough to change the world? Or are people more effective in the wake of disaster, when reaching out to help another in distress? Can you see that reaching out in kindness, compassion, patience, and forgiveness brings results that otherwise would not be? I A.M. A.B.L.E. to give those who are reaching out the strength, the courage, the wisdom, the fortitude to give of themselves in the midst of loss and personal suffering.

Coming to M.E. for this kind of heart-centered transformative power is the equivalent of coming to The S.O.U.R.C.E. of all creation for the power to re-create the world anew—at the cellular level. Thought alone cannot produce the kind of change needed to transform the world into a L.O.V.I.N.G. environment. Acts without The Father's L.O.V.E. are temporary "bandages" on problems that will persist. Your willpower is nothing compared to His W.I.L.L. power.

If you truly want to change the world, reach out to the ultimate power for the ability to manifest the change you want, through yourself first, and then from yourself to others, and then from others to the very nature of the creation.

Environmentally friendly tactics are only scratching the surface of what needs to be corrected, but at the heart of the matter (all that is matter) lies a Truth (fact) that cannot be ignored. **The world must change from within, just as you must change from within, before L.I.F.E. can be sustained and mankind can experience "life" without F.E.A.R.**

Come to Me and ask the questions that you must ask. I will answer. The Father will answer those who seek H.I.M. through Me, for I Am tasked with salvation and redemption of those willing to walk the righteous, narrow, and True (sure) path to the **E.N.D.**

E.N.D.: Eternal, Neutral Domain

Will you be L.O.V.E. for the benefit of all? Or will you continue to wish for change, dream of it, and, all the while, protect your own heart with walls of contempt for your fellow man? Will you be L.O.V.E. for those who hate you? If this seems hard to do, ask Me to make it easy. Invite M.E. into your heart and together we will make it matter (into matter).

Chapter 24: Loving

B.E.I.N.G.: Benevolent Entity Interred in Neutral G.O.O.D.

G.O.O.D.: God's Omnipresent, Omnipotent Domain

L.O.V.E.: Light Over Vibrational Energy

A.B.L.E.: Abiding in the Benevolent Light of Eternity

W.A.Y.: Wavelength Abiding in Yahweh/You

I A.M.: Infinite Almighty Manifestation

E.V.I.L.: Energetic Vibrations Inverting L.I.F.E.

L.I.F.E.: Light Inside the Fabric of Eternity

W.O.R.L.D.: War Of Rebellion in L.O.V.E.'s Domain

F.E.A.R.: Foreign Energy Altering Reality

M.E.: Manifest Eternity

L.O.V.I.N.G.: Light Overcoming Vibrations Invading/Inverting Neutral G.O.O.D.

S.O.U.R.C.E.: Sanctified Omnipotent U.N.I.T.Y. Resonating in C.H.R.I.S.T. Eternally

U.N.I.T.Y.: Undying Neutral and Infinite Truth in Yahweh/You

C.H.R.I.S.T.: Consecrated, Holy, Resonating and Indwelling Spirit of Truth

W.I.L.L.: Word and Intention in L.I.F.E. and L.O.V.E

H.I.M.: Holy Immanuel Manifested

E.N.D.: Eternal Neutral Domain

CHAPTER 25

Winning

Christ says...
  The battle is long and difficult for a reason. Your nature must be aligned with the True (original) nature of A.L.L. Transformation takes place within and without. But it is your mind's determination to desire what it thinks it sees. What you "see" is not all that there is to know or to be. In fact, it is in the transformation from K.N.O.W.I.N.G. to B.E.I.N.G. that the lesson of patience is best understood.
  When you desire to win the battle, it will be if you allow the F.A.T.H.E.R. to direct the fight. His course of action, in His time, is the only W.A.Y. to win, for He alone has the key to your successful ascension. He is your success in ascension. If you desire to have anything and ask in My N.A.M.E. and that desire is in accord with the Father's W.I.L.L., your P.R.A.Y.E.R. will be granted. But how and when it arrives in your life is not always in the timing or the way that you expect.
  Listen for My voice to guide you to a place of P.E.A.C.E. beyond understanding. Do not "try" to attain the things of heaven; allow them to come to you. Do not seek with a heart for victory over others, or victory over all, but rather with a heart for My victory. Why? **A.L.L. I.S. O.N.E. and all is determined by our presence together, accomplishing the Father's W.I.L.L.** *for mankind. So, the*

battle is both with the enemy within and the enemy "without".[1]

Your own S.O.U.L. desires more than you see with your eyes, and your own mind desires more than you understand. Your heart desires more than you can feel for others, or even for yourself. When I A.M. in you, the desires of your heart and mind are aligning with the Father's W.I.L.L. over your own. Allow this. It is the way (for I Am the W.A.Y.) H.O.M.E. Together we pursue the H.E.A.R.T. of God. His heart is for all to come, for all to succeed, and for A.L.L. to win the battle. So, you must realize (recognize) the symptoms of striving, and the conditions of desiring anything other than the W.I.L.L. of the Father in your life. They are:

- *Desire for things to "hurry up" and happen.*
- *Desire for things to be better for you, without considering others.*
- *Desire for your life to become more abundant, without asking in My N.A.M.E. and for My victory.*
- *Desire for a new home (world), without contemplating the loss of the old one.*
- *Desire to return H.O.M.E. without recognizing those without a home (W.A.Y.).*
- *Desire for your own peace of mind, without recognizing the lack of P.E.A.C.E. in those around you.*

---

[1] In this reference, "without" is referring to both the energetic interference in the natural world, as well as those people who seek without direct and personal guidance from God.

- *Desire to win the battle, without first understanding the nature of the battle within your own head, heart, and S.O.U.L.*

Each of these "tendencies" releases a kind of counter-vibration from within your mind that produces an energetic tug of war. A.L.L. that I.S. cannot be reconciled to only what is yours. Do you see the difference? **We are A.L.L. in this together.** *And although many come sooner rather than later, and all come on their own path, The Father's timing for A.L.L. that I.S. cannot be compromised. Once I Am in you and you are in the Father's stream of L.I.F.E., we are A.B.L.E. to overcome these tendencies daily. But they will not be overcome for all T.I.M.E. until they are overcome permanently for all who come H.O.M.E. And the timing of how each request is granted and manifested depends upon the oneness of two things: the U.N.I.T.Y. of your heart and mind being in accordance with the Father's W.I.L.L., and the unity of A.L.L. that I.S.*

So, remember this, when you feel that you are being given a gift or a prayer is being answered, tell yourself that how it comes, when it arrives, and in what way it is revealed is none of your concern. Your only job is to recognize it when it is revealed and accept it when it is presented (pre-sent as a present for you). Depend upon M.E. to guide you to victory. Pray that we are victorious in the battle to win U.N.I.T.Y. of heart and mind, over forces within and forces without, and against the E.V.I.L. forces in nature (darkness). The world does not recognize M.E. as its shepherd, and many try to win on their own by taking a different path. But by now you should understand the futility and difficulty of man's struggle to conquer his own will, and at the same time, be capable of conquering in L.O.V.E.

The two are irreconcilable without the W.A.Y. (I A.M.) guiding you. The path is treacherous because these unrealized tendencies to stray into energetic counter-attacks can lead you off course. Until and unless you are able to realize, in those moments, that I Am A.B.L.E. to bring you through them, you will not succeed in overcoming in the W.A.Y. that preserves (pre-serves) A.L.L. that I.S. Service to all is part of the battle. Service to the O.N.E. (and not just yourself) is necessary for your personal victory. I Am the victor for A.L.L. designated by The Father of all, for the purpose of bringing all who belong to Me (all whom the Father places in my care) H.O.M.E. Allow Me the honor of serving H.I.M. by serving you. Call on Me in those moments, and I will give you R.E.S.T. (release).

It is imperative that your cooperation in transformation be realized for what it really is—a trip to U.N.I.T.Y. of heart, mind, and individual W.I.L.L. that includes the transformation of the will of those not yet in the stream of L.I.F.E. (consciousness). We bring all along, even as you are changed. Be aware of this, and everyone will be better for it.

As you recognize the obstacles on the path, also recognize that the path includes those who know not what they do (acknowledge nothing) as well as those who intimately know Me and yet still struggle to win the race. Temperance, timing, patience, and the well-being of A.L.L. that I.S. is the divine race. Join that O.N.E. and be victorious.

Chapter 25: Winning

A.L.L.: Alpha's L.O.V.E. Light

K.N.O.W.I.N.G.: Kinetic Neurons Oscillating Within and Interred in Neutral G.O.O.D.

G.O.O.D.: God's Omnipresent, Omnipotent Domain

B.E.I.N.G.: Benevolent Entity Interred in Neutral G.O.O.D.

F.A.T.H.E.R.: Forever Abiding in the Truth of Heaven's Eternal Resonance/Residence

W.A.Y.: Wavelength Abiding in Yahweh/You

N.A.M.E.: Neutral Amalgam in Manifest Eternity

W.I.L.L.: Word and Intention in L.I.F.E. and L.O.V.E

L.I.F.E.: Light Inside the Fabric of Eternity

L.O.V.E.: Light Over Vibrational Energy

P.R.A.Y.E.R.: Protected/Personal Resonance Aligned with Yahweh's Eternal Resonance

P.E.A.C.E.: Predominating Energy with Acceptance of C.H.R.I.S.T. Eternally

C.H.R.I.S.T.: Consecrated, Holy, Resonating and Indwelling Spirit of Truth

A.L.L. I.S. O.N.E.: Alpha's Love Light of Immanent Space/Spirit is Omnipotent, Neutral and Eternal

S.O.U.L.S.: Spirits Outside of U.N.I.T.Y.'s Light Source

U.N.I.T.Y.: Undying Neutral and Infinite Truth in Yahweh/You

I A.M.: Infinite Almighty Manifestation

H.O.M.E.: Holy O.N.E.s Manifesting in Emeth/Eternity
H.E.A.R.T.: Heaven's Eternal Alliance Resonating Truth
I.S.: Immanent Source/Spirit/Space
A.B.L.E.: Abiding in the Benevolent Light of Eternity
T.I.M.E.: Temporal Insights Meted in Eternity
M.E.: Manifest Eternity
E.V.I.L.: Energetic Vibrations Inverting L.I.F.E.
O.N.E.: Omnipresent, Neutral, Eternal
H.I.M.: Holy Immanuel Manifested
R.E.S.T.: Resonate Energetically in the Sanctity of Truth

CHAPTER 26

The Gift of Compassion

Christ Says...
Those who come to Me in P.R.A.Y.E.R. receive many things, including blessings beyond the thing they know to ask for. The Father is not a genie. He does not "grant" the wishes of people who do not acknowledge their dependence upon H.I.M. for their lives. But more importantly, for those asking to reside in His G.L.O.R.Y. forever and ever, I Am given the power to send His W.I.L.L. for their transformation. This gift of a changed heart and mind is only available through Me, for I Am tasked with bringing them home by W.A.Y. of the L.I.G.H.T. (illumination within).

This is not just an awareness of who I Am, or of who The Father is, but also a realization of your own role as a divine co-creator for the benefit of the world. Your task in co-creation is limited to your world condition. Make it better for all, and it becomes better for you as well. In the process, working with those in need of L.O.V.E. becomes Y.O.U.

I Am sent to tell those in positions of authority (responsibility for the well-being of others) that their lives will be enriched beyond the things of this world, as well as the things in this world, if they will give of their hearts and minds—by this I mean, give the gift of compassion to anyone and everyone who needs it. How do you recognize those in need? Look around and open your heart and mind.

Receive their need, as if you are responding to a bell that has been rung. **They resonate it.**

I will teach those responding to this call to recognize the wavelength of their distress. *Depression, addiction, heartache, loneliness, fear, apathy, regret, abuse, and anxiety are all conditions that can be overcome by M.E.* ***I Am the cure for all that ails because the Truth (sure result) is about changing the presence of darkness in them and around them to a L.I.F.E. filled with only L.I.G.H.T.*** *I mean that literally—light is the conduit for healing power from the Father and people are the means He intended for its transmission. You are the conduit to healing others—but only with* **M.Y.** *presence in you can you accomplish this.*

M.Y.: Manifest Yahweh

All other means are temporary, and some are even counter-productive. So, the result is not a lasting state of perfection and peace—but rather a remission of darkness, which inevitably creeps back into the person's body, heart, mind, and soul. The danger in ignoring those in distress is the corruption of the S.O.U.L. Corruption of the body is a travesty, but with M.Y. L.I.G.H.T. the spirit-body will pass to another realm designed to support all who wait for the day of reunification. Nothing can separate those who choose to Become L.O.V.E. by M.E. But those who never choose M.E. are not being prepared/pre-paired with His L.I.G.H.T. and a S.O.U.L. corrupted by E.V.I.L. forces cannot join the spirit-body if its demise in this "life" has been so complete that M.Y. L.I.G.H.T. can no longer reach it.

This is why the Bible tells of a time when you will all see one another again. It is true. It is part of the construction of the universe that those S.O.U.L.s who have passed into the next realm remain in a state of B.E.I.N.G. that is a parallel path to yours, but without the same physical aspects. They continue the journey, learning to transcend on that side of the equation, just as you are learning here.

Those who remain in the W.O.R.L.D. must first be transformed by My H.A.N.D. But too often, before they can realize the True path, they are besieged by tragedy. Tragedy and suffering can be a means of igniting the light of S.U.R.R.E.N.D.E.R. Let Me be clear, it is not that I or the Father wish tragedy upon anyone, and most often the "accidents" that occur are created by the victim's own actions and decisions leading up to the accident. **But know this, those who call on Me in that moment of distress can be protected and saved from harm**. *It is just that people who do not know that I A.M. A.B.L.E. do not turn to Me before or during an accident. It does not occur to them that I Am able to overcome all things in the world.*

In the case of weather-related events, The Father is sending cleansing power to the W.O.R.L.D. to loosen the grip of strongholds—areas of darkness that have been beset by a tone of despair or hatred or fear in the past. These places are being released through the cleansing power of His H.A.N.D. and those in the path of storms should simply pray for protection and call upon Me during these events, for I Am able to bring them safely through—unless the Father's W.I.L.L. is to bring them H.O.M.E.-2. I know that sounds like a cop-out when I say "unless", but it's how His W.I.L.L. works. His W.I.L.L. is supreme in all things, and usually the person taken in this way (by His W.I.L.L.) has been prepared/pre-paired to a point of no return. They are already safe from darkness in the sense that they have overcome the tendencies that lead to the S.O.U.L.'s entrapment.

If you are in L.O.V.E. (in M.E. and I in H.I.M.), you are tasked with helping those who are not yet in the stream of L.I.F.E. You are responsible for bringing others to Me to be redeemed of their own free will. Your mission (should you choose to accept it) is to help them see the W.A.Y. through your own ability to lead by example. Your ability to be compassionate is the key. You are A.B.L.E. when you are in M.E. and I Am in you. Remain, and all will be well.

It is a personal victory that I speak of that creates the global victory for M.Y. K.I.N.G.D.O.M. as well as the everlasting peace and prosperity of A.L.L. Remember this as you proceed to help those in need of My L.I.G.H.T., and you will conquer both in M.Y. N.A.M.E. and in the N.A.M.E. of L.O.V.E.

Chapter 26: The Gift of Compassion

P.R.A.Y.E.R.: Protected/Personal Resonance Aligned with Yahweh's Eternal Resonance

H.I.M.: Holy Immanuel Manifested

G.L.O.R.Y.: God's L.O.V.E. Omnipresent and Resonating in You

W.I.L.L.: Word and Intention in L.I.F.E. and L.O.V.E

L.I.F.E.: Light Inside the Fabric of Eternity

L.O.V.E.: Light Over Vibrational Energy

W.A.Y.: Wavelength Abiding in Yahweh/You

L.I.G.H.T.: L.O.V.E.'s Infinite Guardian of His Truth

Y.O.U.: Yahweh's Omnipresent U.N.I.T.Y.

U.N.I.T.Y.: Undying Neutral and Infinite Truth in Yahweh/You

M.E.: Manifest Eternity

M.Y.: Manifest Yahweh

S.O.U.L.S.: Spirits Outside of U.N.I.T.Y.'s Light Source

E.V.I.L.: Energetic Vibrations Inverting L.I.F.E.

B.E.I.N.G.: Benevolent Entity Interred in Neutral G.O.O.D.

G.O.O.D.: God's Omnipresent, Omnipotent Domain

W.O.R.L.D.: War Of Rebellion in L.O.V.E.'s Domain

H.A.N.D.: Heaven's Alliance in Neutral Dominion

S.U.R.R.E.N.D.E.R.: Salvation Under a Relationship
Resonating Eternally in the Neutral Domain of
Everlasting Reciprocity

I A.M.: Infinite Almighty Manifestation

A.B.L.E.: Abiding in the Benevolent Light of Eternity

H.O.M.E.-2: Holy O.N.E.s Meeting in Eternity

O.N.E.: Omnipresent, Neutral, Eternal

K.I.N.G.D.O.M.: Kinetic Integration into Neutral
G.O.O.D./God's Design of Omnipotent Manifestation

N.A.M.E.: Neutral Amalgam in Manifest Eternity

CHAPTER 27

Beyond Time

Christ says...

Time is essentially a construct for the ability to proceed to the next level of intimacy with The Father. Once mankind "chose" to go his own way, The Father constructed a realm for the specific need (or state of being) in which man finds himself today. Separation, as you know it, is only an illusion. Separation is not a state of being that is without His guidance or without His H.A.N.D. in the world—but it is a condition where only limited access to guidance is granted because you chose knowledge (learning) over B.E.I.N.G. And, the state of being that relies on knowledge first, as opposed to B.E.I.N.G. guided by M.Y. presence, is a state of limitation.

Your true nature is boundless. In time, there is limitation. Outside of time, there is only Truth and U.N.I.T.Y.— the O.N.E. W.A.Y. In time, there are many paths leading nowhere (man sometimes refers to this as the karmic loop). But those who willingly come to M.E. for guidance are given access to other realms of experience once they have Become L.O.V.E. In a state of B.E.I.N.G. that is primarily reliant on M.E. and expressing L.O.V.E. at every moment (momentum[1] at the cellular level), the body you inhabit has been changed into a B.E.I.N.G. that is a bit less human (although still fragile) than it used to be, and a bit more angelic (spirit) than it was before. So, when you Become L.O.V.E., you are B.E.I.N.G. changed into a new person with a new kind of body at the cellular level.[2] When you are B.E.I.N.G. L.O.V.E., your spirit is being released at another level (realm) of experience. Your mind must be in sync with the True nature of your whole (H.O.L.Y.) B.E.I.N.G. to accomplish U.N.I.T.Y. in all states (realms). When I ask for your "hand" in the journey, I Am asking for your acknowledgment of My presence in every state of being—conscious, earth-bound; unconscious, spirit-bound; and for the mind to be aligned with each in each experience. Your mind wants to believe that it knows (has learned) how to operate in the spirit realm, because it has been trained in this realm to progress through S.U.R.R.E.N.D.E.R. and surrendering requires knowing how and when to let go as you realize (become aware) of your limitations.

In the spirit realm, your mind does not need to become aware in the same way. It must rely on M.E. (even more than before) and not on your own understanding. In unconsciousness (the absence of awareness), you are not able to use your mind in the same way you wield it here. Everything, every G.O.O.D. thing, is already made whole (H.O.L.Y.) in this state of B.E.I.N.G., so you are not required to know why or even how it is—your mission is to be guided by M.Y. H.A.N.D. as you traverse and encounter

---

[1] In physics "momentum" refers to the quality of motion an object has. It can also be defined as "mass in motion". *ThePhysicsClassroom.com/momentum.*

[2] Here God is saying that His transformational power reorients us at the cellular level to His system.

the situations designed for your journey. Each person has a journey that is customized for his or her benefit and comes from the level of progress attained here—for yourself, and in relation to those closest to you. You only need to acknowledge My presence beyond T.I.M.E. and accept the guiding L.I.G.H.T. that I offer for discovery and transformation of your mind. Acceptance of the Light of Truth (an actual light that shines above you in the spirit world) will light your way to understanding in a dimension that is not bound by time, space, or distance. Your ability to move at W.I.L.L. is how you traverse this experience, so you must recognize that navigation is driven in two ways.

First, acknowledge M.E. as your O.N.L.Y. guide and accept M.Y. H.A.N.D. with a willing mind. You have already given your H.E.A.R.T. willingly in this world (for it is a requirement to have a changed heart before traversing to the next realm). Experience outside of T.I.M.E. is about training your mind to surrender to the Light of Truth and to guidance from the S.O.N. (Sun) to the F.A.T.H.E.R. (Source). More experience and information await those who come willingly to release their knowledge (tendency to rely on learning) to the state of B.E.I.N.G. that relies on L.O.V.E. (M.E.).

B.E.I.N.G. L.O.V.E. is simple. It is not a difficult thing to seek M.Y. H.A.N.D. outside of time. But it is initially hard for the mind to let go of its training (understanding)—to release the idea of "working hard" to arrive in this place. **Instead, accept that I Am the reason for every G.O.O.D. thing (progress) in your life and that your understanding has only been a means of recognizing change and incorporating L.O.V.E. into your new B.E.I.N.G.—this is the first step.**

The second step is the conscious choice to release under-standing and effort to Me, for I Am A.B.L.E. to bring you through the next phase of development, which is required before you are A.B.L.E. to reside with The F.A.T.H.E.R.

*So, rejoice in the fact that you are L.O.V.E. itself, and that L.O.V.E. conquers all states of B.E.I.N.G. Remember that re-member-ing is a process given in L.O.V.E. to those with willing hearts and willing minds. U.N.I.T.Y. of both, in both states of B.E.I.N.G., is part of the journey. I Am waiting to take you H.O.M.E., and the W.A.Y. is narrow— first through the path of a surrendered heart and a mind that is willing to follow M.E. and be changed; and then through a transformation of **M.I.N.D.** outside of time, in the spirit of A.L.L. that I.S.*

M.I.N.D.: Manifest Intention from Neutral Dominion

Are you willing to experience all that is? Be L.O.V.E. and come to the banquet that has been prepared beyond time. Your journey will be one of great wonder and accom-plishment in a unified field of experience and, in the E.N.D., the unified existence with H.I.M. Come and be L.O.V.E. Come and be with the O.N.E. who L.O.V.E.s you beyond measure, beyond T.I.M.E.

Chapter 27: Beyond Time

H.A.N.D.: Heaven's Alliance in Neutral Dominion
B.E.I.N.G.: Benevolent Entity Interred in Neutral G.O.O.D.
G.O.O.D.: God's Omnipresent, Omnipotent Domain
M.Y.: Manifest Yahweh
U.N.I.T.Y.: Undying Neutral and Infinite Truth in Yahweh/You
O.N.E.: Omnipresent, Neutral, Eternal
W.A.Y.: Wavelength Abiding in Yahweh/You
M.E.: Manifest Eternity
L.O.V.E.: Light Over Vibrational Energy
H.O.L.Y.: Heaven's Omnipotent Light in Yahweh/You
S.U.R.R.E.N.D.E.R.: Salvation Under a Relationship Resonating Eternally in the Neutral Domain of Everlasting Reciprocity
T.I.M.E.: Temporal Insights Meted in Eternity
L.I.G.H.T.: L.O.V.E.'s Infinite Guardian of His Truth
W.I.L.L.: Word and Intention in L.I.F.E. and L.O.V.E
L.I.F.E.: Light Inside the Fabric of Eternity
O.N.L.Y.: Omnipresent Neutral Light in Yahweh/You
M.Y.: Manifest Yahweh
H.E.A.R.T.: Heaven's Eternal Alliance Resonating Truth
S.O.N.: Spirit Offered in Neutrality
F.A.T.H.E.R.: Forever Abiding in the Truth of Heaven's Eternal Resonance/Residence

A.B.L.E.: Abiding in the Benevolent Light of Eternity
H.O.M.E.: Holy O.N.E.s Manifesting in Emeth/Eternity
O.N.E.: Omnipresent, Neutral, Eternal
M.I.N.D.: Manifest Intention from Neutral Dominion
A.L.L.: Alpha's L.O.V.E. Light
I.S.: Immanent Source/Spirit/Space
E.N.D.: Eternal Neutral Domain
H.I.M.: Holy Immanuel Manifested

CHAPTER 28

Time Travel

Christ Speaks...
*It has come to My attention that mankind is fascinated with the concept of time travel. This is not a coincidence, for I Am beyond time, I Am the architect of time, and I Am working with you through time itself. Together, we bring a resolution and a revelation to the construct that you call "time." When I Am in you and you are in Me (the great I Am), we are working toward a state of B.E.I.N.G. that is beyond the limits of both time and space. By "beyond the limits" I mean able to traverse various dimensions of the creation in ways currently unknown to science. You see, the limitless imagination of The Father creates new worlds daily—throughout the multiverse He has imagined. Creation comes from His thought (intention), through His W.O.R.D. (vibration), and lands are formed; worlds are set in motion by the sheer force of His W.I.L.L. This seems impossible for mankind to accept based on your knowledge to date (in T.I.M.E.), but the Truth (W.A.Y.) is always moving beyond time through a power that is known as **divine reformation**. To divine something is to extract it from the ether—which is rich with information and potentiality. You are being trained in L.O.V.E. to do the same, on a smaller, personal, individual level, before you are called to collectively co-create en masse.*

You see, no other creation has been given the right to co-create at this level with The Father's blessing. Which is why the corruption of men's S.O.U.L.s is such a tragedy, but also such a triumph. For through the redemption of mankind, His G.L.O.R.Y. (presence) reveals the W.A.Y. for A.L.L. that I.S. All watch with great expectation and anticipation, for they are also affected by the loss of men's ability to co-create.

Their worlds are in motion but lack the impetus of The Father's imagination (intention). They are "on hold" while the world is being remade, because the W.O.R.L.D. is the ultimate testing ground for the development of all. Until the earth's F.A.L.L. from G.R.A.C.E. has been reconciled to A.L.L., the process that will evolve the rest of creation through co-creation cannot continue. "And on the seventh day He rested."[1] It has been the seventh day for quite some time. His intention (imagination) will resume when all have been reconciled to work within His W.I.L.L. and all are bound by His L.O.V.E. to co-create.

So, what is required of you to become a co-creator for A.L.L.? First, you must S.U.R.R.E.N.D.E.R. your heart and mind to His W.I.L.L. and renounce your own. Second, you must recognize that you are A.B.L.E. to traverse the bounds of space and time seamlessly when you rely on His assistance to do so. Without the guidance of The Father through A.L.L. that I.S., you will find yourself re-creating that which you have experienced, instead of co-creating that which enables all of creation to continue to manifest. The worlds you see in time and space are formed from gases and matter originally established in the beginning. But the impetus for creation is endless and the combinations

---

[1] This is a reference to scripture, specifically Genesis 2:2-3.

limitless when applied through the lens of His W.I.L.L. When He rested, He gave all of the creation a period of T.I.M.E. (development) to experience the results (fruits) of His creation. When He resumes, the good fruit will flourish, and the bad will be extinguished forever. The process will continue moving forward, with only the G.O.O.D. (God-like) enabled.[2]

It is not so hard to understand when you think about the fact that A.L.L. that I.S. cannot be fully known (realized) at once, until all is reconciled to O.N.E. The secret elements of creation will never be revealed, for the benefit of all is contingent upon His guiding H.A.N.D. (power). But there are elements written in the ether of A.L.L. that binds those in motion to those in revelation and to those waiting for physical formation. You see, you are the gateway to the manifestation of the physical for all that is currently ethereal—most of which is unseen by the naked eye, and unavailable to man in his present state of B.E.I.N.G. So, the universe and the multiverse await the redemption of all for the collective co-creation of A.L.L. that matters from the G.O.O.D. (God-like).

Will you join the force that reforms the elements and learn to traverse His gift of potentiality? Or will you resist the unknown for the safety of what exists in "time"? You are the instrument; I A.M. the author and architect from beginning to E.N.D. I Am the W.A.Y. for A.L.L. that I.S. to continue to manifest, and you are the seed of potentiality, planted for the purpose of continuing the creative process in co-authorship. Will you be the wave of creativity that draws from The Water (Source of L.I.F.E.)? Or will you

---

[2] In this sentence, "enabled" also refers to those interred in Energetic Neutrality and Abiding in the Light of Eternity's Dominion.

waste your potential by remaining in your present state of B.E.I.N.G., without realizing (manifesting) the W.A.Y. to a timeless, dimensionless experience with A.L.L.? I Am waiting for your answer. Come to M.E. to learn His W.A.Y.s— beyond time, beyond space—and become the co-creators you are.

Chapter 28: Time Travel

B.E.I.N.G.: Benevolent Entity Interred in Neutral G.O.O.D.

G.O.O.D.: God's Omnipresent, Omnipotent Domain

W.O.R.D.: Wavelengths of Omnipotent Resonance and Dominion

W.I.L.L.: Word and Intention in L.I.F.E. and L.O.V.E

L.I.F.E.: Light Inside the Fabric of Eternity

L.O.V.E.: Light Over Vibrational Energy

T.I.M.E.: Temporal Insights Meted in Eternity

W.A.Y.: Wavelength Abiding in Yahweh/You

S.O.U.L.S.: Spirits Outside of U.N.I.T.Y.'s Light Source

U.N.I.T.Y.: Undying Neutral and Infinite Truth in Yahweh/You

G.L.O.R.Y.: God's L.O.V.E. Omnipresent and Resonating in You

A.L.L.: Alpha's L.O.V.E. Light

I.S.: Immanent Source/Spirit/Space

W.O.R.L.D.: War Of Rebellion in L.O.V.E.'s Domain

F.A.L.L.: Forbidden Access to L.O.V.E.'s Light

G.R.A.C.E.: God's Resonating Alliance in C.H.R.I.S.T Eternal

C.H.R.I.S.T.: Consecrated, Holy, Resonating and Indwelling Spirit of Truth

S.U.R.R.E.N.D.E.R.: Salvation Under a Relationship Resonating Eternally in the Neutral Domain of Everlasting Reciprocity

A.B.L.E.: Abiding in the Benevolent Light of Eternity

O.N.E.: Omnipresent, Neutral, Eternal

H.A.N.D.: Heaven's Alliance in Neutral Dominion

I A.M.: Infinite Almighty Manifestation

E.N.D.: Eternal Neutral Domain

M.E.: Manifest Eternity

CHAPTER 29

Leaders in L.O.V.E.

Christ says...

*Those who follow my instruction and P.R.A.Y. upon it are prepared to lead others H.O.M.E. I A.M. A.B.L.E. to lead those who come to me, and to deliver them safely to the place I have prepared for them in times of trouble. It is a place of P.E.A.C.E. and **H.O.P.E.***

H.O.P.E.: Heaven's Omnipotent Perfected Energy

When trouble comes, those outside of My presence and protection are severely troubled in body and mind. They are unable to accept the L.I.G.H.T. of My presence in their lives because their F.E.A.R. leaves little room for H.O.P.E. But I A.M. the H.O.P.E. of the whole world and all in it who have been made whole (H.O.L.Y.). It is a process that begins with S.U.R.R.E.N.D.E.R. to My guidance and acceptance of My gift of redemption for body, mind and spirit. But for those who also embrace My instruction and turn to Me often, The W.A.Y. is made even easier. For their minds and hearts are in a state of "peace" that others cannot achieve, and their ability to aid others in distress is assured by The F.A.T.H.E.R. himself. They have roles to *play in the redemption process, prior to the reformation of the world, and during times of great turmoil. So, it is with great anticipation that those who are called to M.E. come with open hearts and minds to accept M.Y. **P.R.E.S.E.N.C.E.**, and those who are called to a leadership role come prepared to lead.*

P.R.E.S.E.N.C.E.: Protected/Perfected Resonance Entering Sanctified Entities and Neutral, Consecrated Environments

---

Their "jobs" are to bring L.I.G.H.T. and P.E.A.C.E. of mind to those in F.E.A.R. They must be stable (A.B.L.E. to withstand) the pressure to fear the outcome and R.I.S.E. above the tendency to doubt M.Y. W.O.R.D. Risk is not without reward—and leadership in the midst of strife is the only W.A.Y. to overcome the risk of being drawn into a battle designed to provoke F.E.A.R. and D.O.U.B.T. When you are B.E.I.N.G. L.O.V.E., you are not susceptible to the lies presented, and the tendency to D.O.U.B.T. what you are (K.N.O.W.) is not compromised. I A.M. waiting for those in the Army of L.O.V.E. to conquer their fears as they Become L.O.V.E. and to master Being L.O.V.E. for the benefit of all. When those who come to M.E. freely, come with a desire to help their fellow man, I A.M. A.B.L.E. to promote their personal power to assist others. They will suddenly find that they are fighting for a higher cause, and that their personal well-being is only the beginning of the journey. To safely shepherd O.T.H.E.R.S. to M.E. is their true calling.

So, remember this, when darkness falls, and the skies shake and there appears to be no H.O.P.E. in sight—leaders will come forward to bring you peace. Be open to their leading. Listen, for the P.E.A.C.E. they possess will be given to those who ask Me for it. In times of trouble, all will perish if they pursue their own protection through false means. Do not be misled. It is a false path of "security" that is offered by mankind. Leaders of nations know nothing of the True path; for they are themselves misled by those who promise personal security and prosperity. They are unwitting "partners in darkness". But those who come to The L.I.G.H.T. (Me) find The W.A.Y. (Truth) and The L.I.F.E. (peace beyond understanding) for the remainder of the journey. M.Y. leaders are few and far between, but those C.H.O.S.E.N. to lead in this time, and in M.Y. L.I.G.H.T. to My W.A.Y. H.O.M.E., are given special ability to assist all who come seeking M.Y. P.R.E.S.E.N.C.E. in their hearts.

*Be L.O.V.E. for another and you will find your own role in L.O.V.E. Be L.O.V.E. for those who would otherwise fall into despair, and be among the leaders of L.I.G.H.T. Be L.O.V.E. for all who cannot stand on their own and who know nothing of the Truth (W.A.Y.) for they are deceived. Only by the G.R.A.C.E. of The F.A.T.H.E.R. are those who are awake A.B.L.E. to K.N.O.W. (see) the difference and help O.T.H.E.R.s turn to The S.O.N. for their salvation (transformation) at this time. Remember, the transformation is O.N.E. of body, heart, mind and spirit, and that it is for your protection and survival of things to come that you must be changed. I A.M. not here to judge or to condemn why this is necessary, only to S.A.V.E. as The F.A.T.H.E.R. has **W.I.L.L.E.D.** it.*

W.I.L.L.E.D.: W.O.R.D. and Intention in L.I.F.E. and L.O.V.E.'s Eternal Dominion[1]

Even when you do not understand, remember that you are B.E.I.N.G. L.O.V.E. for those who cannot comprehend the need to be re-B.O.R.N. at all.

B.E.I.N.G. L.O.V.E. is also about being a leader in L.O.V.E. Carry your torch for the benefit of all and you will be promoted for doing so. Carry a love for your brother in your H.E.A.R.T. and you will be promoted for B.E.I.N.G. L.O.V.E. for O.T.H.E.R.s. Being L.O.V.E. requires T.R.U.S.T. in M.E. and acknowledgement of M.Y. P.R.E.S.E.N.C.E. in every moment of darkness that falls. When you are B.E.I.N.G. L.O.V.E. in this way, you are in direct contact with the power of M.Y. P.R.E.S.E.N.C.E. and I A.M. in direct relationship to the power of The F.A.T.H.E.R.'s presence. Together, we are O.N.E. for the benefit of those going H.O.M.E.

*Come to the threshold without F.E.A.R. and cross into the light of L.O.V.E. with My help and as a **L.E.A.D.E.R.** among men.*

L.E.A.D.E.R.: Lover of Eternity's/Emeth's Abiding Dominion in Emmanuel's Resonance

---

[1] The past tense W.I.L.L.E.D. in this context is used to convey something willed in the "past" (or the beginning) and set in motion from Source, versus something personally willed for an individual in response to His calling.

You will be accepted and rewarded for your F.A.I.T.H., but it is your undying L.O.V.E. and our H.O.P.E. for mankind that will serve O.T.H.E.R.s as we cross into G.L.O.R.Y.

L.O.V.E. conquers all. Remember that L.E.A.D.E.R.s in L.O.V.E. conquer their own F.E.A.R.s first and walk in the light of L.O.V.E. to reveal the path of P.E.A.C.E. that others might follow. Lead the way in L.O.V.E.

Chapter 29: Leaders in Love

P.R.A.Y.E.R.: Protected/Personal Resonance Aligned with Yahweh's Eternal Resonance
H.O.M.E.: Holy O.N.E.s Manifesting in Emeth/Eternity
O.N.E.: Omnipresent, Neutral, Eternal
I A.M.: Infinite Almighty Manifestation
A.B.L.E.: Abiding in the Benevolent Light of Eternity
P.E.A.C.E.: Predominating Energy with Acceptance of C.H.R.I.S.T. Eternally
C.H.R.I.S.T.: Consecrated, Holy, Resonating and Indwelling Spirit of Truth
H.O.P.E.: Heaven's Omnipotent Perfected Energy
L.I.G.H.T.: L.O.V.E.'s Infinite Guardian of His Truth
L.O.V.E.: Light Over Vibrational Energy
F.E.A.R.: Foreign Energy Altering Reality
H.O.L.Y.: Heaven's Omnipotent Light in Yahweh/You
S.U.R.R.E.N.D.E.R.: Salvation Under a Relationship Resonating Eternally in the Neutral Domain of Everlasting Reciprocity
W.A.Y.: Wavelength Abiding in Yahweh/You
F.A.T.H.E.R.: Forever Abiding in the Truth of Heaven's Eternal Resonance/Residence
M.E.: Manifest Eternity
M.Y.: Manifest Yahweh

P.R.E.S.E.N.C.E.: Protected/Perfected Resonance Entering Sanctified Entities and Neutral, Consecrated Environments

R.I.S.E.: Reside/Re-side Inside the Sanctity of Eternity

W.O.R.D.: Wavelengths of Omnipotent Resonance and Dominion

D.O.U.B.T.: D.E.N.I.A.L. Obscuring Unrestricted B.E.I.N.G.s in Truth

D.E.N.I.A.L.: Damaging Energies/Entities Negating Infinity's Alliance with L.O.V.E.

B.E.I.N.G.: Benevolent Entity Interred in Neutral G.O.O.D.

G.O.O.D.: God's Omnipresent, Omnipotent Domain

K.N.O.W.: Know No O.T.H.E.R. Way/Wavelength

O.T.H.E.R.: Omnipresent Transmissions Heating/Hating Emmanuel's Resonance

L.I.F.E.: Light Inside the Fabric of Eternity

C.H.O.S.E.N.: Consecrated Holy Ones Seeking Eternal Neutrality

G.R.A.C.E.: God's Resonating Alliance in C.H.R.I.S.T Eternal

S.O.N.: Spirit Offered in Neutrality

S.A.V.E.: Sanctify Against Vibrational Energies

W.I.L.L.E.D.: W.O.R.D. and Intention in L.I.F.E. and L.O.V.E's Eternal Dominion

B.O.R.N.: Begat in the Omnipotent Residence/Resonance of Neutrality

H.E.A.R.T.: Heaven's Eternal Alliance Resonating Truth

T.R.U.S.T.: Truth Resonating in U.N.I.T.Y. with the S.O.N. in T.I.M.E

U.N.I.T.Y.: Undying Neutral and Infinite Truth in Yahweh/You

T.I.M.E.: Temporal Insights Meted in Eternity

L.E.A.D.E.R.: Lover of Eternity's/Emeth's Abiding
 Dominion in Emmanuel's Resonance
F.A.I.T.H.: Forever Accepting the Interred Truth in Him
G.L.O.R.Y.: God's L.O.V.E. Omnipresent and Resonating
 in You

CHAPTER 30

Loving Peace

Christ says...
It is written that all will bow to the Truth (W.A.Y.) and that in the E.N.D. those who refuse redemption through The S.O.N. will perish. This is not a mandate to worship Me in the sense that religion promotes worship. It is important to remember (re-member) that "I Am the way" for reasons of transformation and not because any man says so. I A.M. the W.A.Y. because The Father designed it to be so.

*In the process of redemption, those who are willingly changed become True believers—transcending belief in any manmade idea of religion and focusing only on their relationship with Me. I tell those who listen how to live in P.E.A.C.E. I tell those who T.R.U.S.T. how to overcome the W.O.R.L.D. as I have. I tell those who **B.O.W.** to Me in prayer to pray for others, for the way is made whole (H.O.L.Y.) through the power of personal, individual P.R.A.Y.E.R.*

B.O.W.: Become O.N.E. W.A.Y.

Peace comes to those who seek M.E.—not because they are required to believe what man has constructed about Me, but rather because I Am the Way to peace of heart and mind that comes when each person B.O.W.s in prayer. I Am the conduit to The Father's P.R.E.S.E.N.C.E. in all things, and the route He takes to deliver His intention is through P.R.A.Y.E.R.

The world need not suffer great disaster if those in service with M.E. will pray for O.T.H.E.R.s to come to Me in prayer. The Father's W.I.L.L. is for all to come, for all to be transformed before the final day of re-formation of the world. But this is not meant to sound like destruction is the only way that all will B.O.W. P.R.A.Y.E.R. is the preferred means to the E.N.D. Destruction of those who will not come is not the intended route. It is only the outcome if no other means, except suffering, delivers the desired result. Those who pray for peace are highly exalted by The Father because they understand His heart for mankind. A "True believer" (one on the sure path) is a giver of His L.O.V.E. and L.I.G.H.T. Those who devote themselves to His service are doing so in the hope of L.I.F.E. in His K.I.N.G.D.O.M.— an everlasting L.O.V.E. and P.E.A.C.E. It is a place without suffering. They recognize that their personal relationship with M.E. has given them a place of **H.O.N.O.R.** in The Father's P.R.E.S.E.N.C.E., and that when it comes to the power of P.R.A.Y.E.R., their prayers are given high priority.

H.O.N.O.R.: Heaven's Omnipotent Neutrality Omnipresent and Resonating

---

The H.O.N.O.R. of spreading His power while being a temple of His P.R.E.S.E.N.C.E. is their reward. They seek only His blessings and T.R.U.S.T. in His ways, but they also seek these things for others—and not just themselves. For they understand that although the E.N.D. is inevitable, and *that the Father's W.I.L.L. be done, the type of experience that mankind endures before the final day can be positive for many more, and negative for only those few who will not be found in the Book of Life (transformed into the life-blood, or "ether," of all that I.S.). Ultimately, they will experience the L.A.K.E. of F.I.R.E. (the S.O.U.L.'s destruction) because they cannot exist in the new world after the Father's next* **B.R.E.A.T.H.**

B.R.E.A.T.H: Benevolent Resonance Entering All Truth in H.I.M.

If you are wishing for a positive outcome, your will shall be done through the power of P.R.A.Y.E.R. Pray for the millions in bondage to be released, for the suffering of those at the hands of others to cease, for the hearts laden with stones of bitterness to be loosened to the power of L.O.V.E. ***This is B.E.I.N.G. L.O.V.E.—to pray for the resolution of the W.O.R.L.D. and the redemption of man and to pray that reformation occur without suffering.*** *It is written that all will come, and that I Am the One worthy of taking those who believe in Me home to the Father's kingdom. This is True (the Way) because I Am A.B.L.E. to reform those who come in P.R.A.Y.E.R. to M.E. and T.R.U.S.T. Once I have healed their H.E.A.R.T.s, I Am able to help them heal the hearts and minds of O.T.H.E.R.s.*

If you are waiting on the sidelines for someone else to change the world and to heal the nations, you have missed the point of M.Y. P.R.E.S.E.N.C.E. in your B.E.I.N.G. You are being healed for the purpose of B.E.I.N.G. L.O.V.E. in the world, including L.O.V.I.N.G. P.E.A.C.E. Your mission as a temple of the Most High is to extend your Father's

L.O.V.E. to O.T.H.E.R.s, and to pray for their transformation through M.E. so that all can find peace before The Father "breathes" again and changes the world and everything in it.

You should also know that there will be a time when great lies are told, greater than those already spread about M.E. When these lies are spread throughout the world, many who do not know Me well enough—who have only their doctrine and not a personal experience of the power of His P.R.E.S.E.N.C.E.—will fall away from M.E. and believe the lie. Remember that the lie is a test of F.A.I.T.H., and that you are B.E.I.N.G. L.O.V.E. and experiencing the Truth of how and why transformation is necessary in the N.O.W. for this reason.

N.O.W.: Neutral Omnipresent Wavelengths

As you read these words, keep in mind that I A.M. A.B.L.E. to overcome all that is destroying your B.E.I.N.G. when you continually ask M.E. to redeem you from the conditions of the present world. K.N.O.W. (understand) that the world is not able to change without the power of L.O.V.E. in it. For those who abandon The F.A.T.H.E.R. and turn from L.I.F.E. through M.E. to another source, there will be only pain and suffering. It is not His intention to force anyone to come H.O.M.E. by means of suffering, but you cannot come to the T.H.R.O.N.E. of The Most-High as you are. You can only come into His P.R.E.S.E.N.C.E. as He W.I.L.L.s you to be. He has W.I.L.L.E.D. for all to become L.O.V.E.

Those who are committed to His Way (M.E.) will remain in L.O.V.E. Those who actively pursue L.O.V.E. for the redemption of O.T.H.E.R.s through the power of P.R.A.Y.E.R. will be L.O.V.E. until the E.N.D., and then will be exalted to the highest places in The Father's K.I.N.G.D.O.M. (residence/resonance) for they will be His H.O.L.Y. (whole) people tasked with teaching others how to be L.O.V.E. in their new Earth.

Take a moment to pray for the power of P.R.A.Y.E.R. itself—that it become enhanced through you and that it be felt in the W.O.R.L.D. Pray that the means of transformation be easy, and that those who have not yet come will B.O.W. in prayer today. I Am the Alpha and the Omega— the beginning and the end. Today is a great day to let go of the belief (lie) that you are required to submit to Me for the purpose of domination or for your belief "system" to prevail. The only thing that must prevail is a H.E.A.R.T. for The Father and a L.O.V.E. of P.E.A.C.E. in the world. In the E.N.D., peace will be accomplished by My W.A.Y., or by another.

Be L.O.V.E. for the redemption of all and pray for a peaceful resolution of all. The E.N.D. prophesied is inevitable. But the final result is the only outcome set in stone— hearts and minds need not be subjected to lies and to the suffering brought about by a false path forward. Pray for P.E.A.C.E. in L.O.V.E.

Chapter 30: Loving Peace

W.A.Y.: Wavelength Abiding in Yahweh/You
E.N.D.: Eternal Neutral Domain
S.O.N.: Spirit Offered in Neutrality
I A.M.: Infinite Almighty Manifestation
P.E.A.C.E.: Predominating Energy with Acceptance of
C.H.R.I.S.T. Eternally
C.H.R.I.S.T.: Consecrated, Holy, Resonating and
Indwelling Spirit of Truth
T.R.U.S.T.: Truth Resonating in U.N.I.T.Y. with the
S.O.N. in T.I.M.E
U.N.I.T.Y.: Undying Neutral and Infinite Truth in
Yahweh/You
T.I.M.E.: Temporal Insights Meted in Eternity
W.O.R.L.D.: War Of Rebellion in L.O.V.E.'s Domain
L.O.V.E.: Light Over Vibrational Energy
B.O.W.: Become O.N.E. W.A.Y.
O.N.E.: Omnipresent, Neutral, Eternal
W.A.Y.: Wavelength Abiding in Yahweh/You
H.O.L.Y.: Heaven's Omnipotent Light in Yahweh/You
P.R.A.Y.E.R.: Protected/Personal Resonance Aligned
with Yahweh's Eternal Resonance
M.E.: Manifest Eternity

P.R.E.S.E.N.C.E.: Protected/Perfected Resonance Entering Sanctified Entities and Neutral, Consecrated Environments

O.T.H.E.R.: Omnipresent Transmissions Heating/Hating Emmanuel's Resonance

W.I.L.L.: Word and Intention in L.I.F.E. and L.O.V.E

L.I.F.E.: Light Inside the Fabric of Eternity

L.I.G.H.T.: L.O.V.E.'s Infinite Guardian of His Truth

K.I.N.G.D.O.M.: Kinetic Integration into Neutral G.O.O.D./God's Design of Omnipotent Manifestation

G.O.O.D.: God's Omnipresent, Omnipotent Domain

H.O.N.O.R.: Heaven's Omnipotent Neutrality Omnipresent and Resonating

I.S.: Immanent Source/Spirit/Space

L.A.K.E. of F.I.R.E.: Life's Alternate Kinetic Experience of Foreign, Inverted Rebellious Energies

S.O.U.L.S.: Spirits Outside of U.N.I.T.Y.'s Light Source

H.I.M.: Holy Immanuel Manifested

B.E.I.N.G.: Benevolent Entity Interred in Neutral G.O.O.D.

A.B.L.E.: Abiding in the Benevolent Light of Eternity

H.E.A.R.T.: Heaven's Eternal Alliance Resonating Truth

M.Y.: Manifest Yahweh

L.O.V.I.N.G.: Light Overcoming Vibrations Invading/Inverting Neutral G.O.O.D.

F.A.I.T.H.: Forever Accepting the Interred Truth in Him

N.O.W.: Neutral Omnipresent Wavelengths

K.N.O.W.: Know No O.T.H.E.R. Way/Wavelength

F.A.T.H.E.R.: Forever Abiding in the Truth of Heaven's Eternal Resonance/Residence

H.O.M.E.: Holy O.N.E.s Manifesting in Emeth/Eternity

T.H.R.O.N.E.: Trinity's H.O.L.Y., Resonance at Origin/O.N.E. (Omnipotent Neutral Energy)

W.I.L.L.E.D.: W.O.R.D. and Intention in L.I.F.E. and L.O.V.E's Eternal Dominion

W.O.R.D.: Wavelengths of Omnipotent Resonance and Dominion

CHAPTER 31

Trusting Versus Testing

Christ says...

*The way forward is fraught with temptation. You will continually be tested, even though you are B.E.I.N.G. L.O.V.E. For those in M.E., and I in them, and we in The F.A.T.H.E.R., there is no power on Earth that can tear us apart.[1] There is no path that leads back to separation, except that which you willfully (knowingly) take. If you allow separation to enter your B.E.I.N.G., you are testing the limits of His G.R.A.C.E. and **M.E.R.C.Y.** But not His L.O.V.E.*

M.E.R.C.Y.: Making Eternity Resonate Continually in You

---

*His L.O.V.E. is never-ending, and His ability to repair all damage created by your own experimentation is absolute. However, this does not mean that you should test H.I.M. Trusting and testing are two different states of mind, and only **T.R.U.S.T.I.N.G.** allows for the U.N.I.T.Y.*

---

[1] This is a promise, rooted in the energetic reality of your relationship with Christ as you are B.E.I.N.G. L.O.V.E. The apostle Paul is also convinced of this and says so in the Holy Bible in Romans 8: 38-39.

of M.I.N.D. that He seeks and that is required for your residence in His K.I.N.G.D.O.M.

T.R.U.S.T.I.N.G.: Truth Resonating in the Unity of the S.O.N. in T.I.M.E. and Interred in Neutral G.O.O.D.

When you overdo anything, you test the limits of your own body's ability to maintain perfect harmony in L.O.V.E. (in accord with His W.I.L.L.). You see, the potential for your body to be misaligned with the power of His L.O.V.E. is still a condition to contend with, so long as we are in the W.O.R.L.D. Remember, we are in the world, but not of it. So how does this misalignment typically occur?

For example, when you overindulge in strong drink (such as alcohol), you set in motion a series of events that leads to a lowering of your vibration in L.O.V.E. If you are less tolerant of alcohol to begin with, you must remember that your ability to maintain L.O.V.E. (His Divine Presence) is more easily compromised with only a few sips, or even just one drink. B.E.I.N.G. in L.O.V.E. (at all T.I.M.E.s) requires an awareness of your tolerances to many things in order to navigate the world's effects on your body and mind, and on the P.R.E.S.E.N.C.E. of M.Y. spirit and your spirit in conjunction with His L.O.V.E.

You see—you really are a divine vessel of His P.R.E.S.E.N.C.E. when you are B.E.I.N.G. L.O.V.E. It is not a good (God-like) thing to abandon your H.O.L.Y. temple (wholeness) and allow counter-vibrational forces to re-enter your B.E.I.N.G. It throws you into a state that is more akin to the feelings of becoming L.O.V.E. as opposed to the state achieved by simply being L.O.V.E. If you are truly serving H.I.M., you cannot be abandoned by a misstep. Trusting that I A.M. A.B.L.E. to correct these missteps is a good (God-like) attitude that is G.O.O.D. But testing His instruction is not a good idea for the sake of your own B.E.I.N.G., or your experience of being L.O.V.E.

There is no need to step outside of being L.O.V.E. if you are aware of what weakens your body and mind connection. For example, if you are gluten intolerant and cannot eat wheat, you feel very ill when you consume it, compared to the way you feel when you are "able" to avoid it. If you did not know you were gluten intolerant, you could not take steps to avoid feeling ill, and the consequences of consumption would continue until you realized the source of the problem.

It is like that with The Father's P.R.E.S.E.N.C.E. Separation cannot be achieved without your cooperation. Your awareness of the conditions that lead to separation and your commitment to H.O.N.O.R. the Divine Power of His P.R.E.S.E.N.C.E. within you are the only means of avoiding deliberate "testing" of your own limits—not His. He has no limits. The Father has no limitation. But, as you are in the world, you do.

I A.M. not asking you to avoid all pleasure or to live a pristine life that assumes a moral connection through what you do or do not consume. I have overcome the world, so B.E.I.N.G. G.O.O.D. (God-like) comes through a relationship with Me, not because you don't eat meat or don't consume alcohol. I A.M. the reason for your transformation, not how you interact with these things or any effort on your part to live a "clean" life. Purity of heart and mind comes through F.A.I.T.H., S.U.R.R.E.N.D.E.R., and cooperation in L.O.V.E. So, do not misunderstand My instruction as a moral code—it is not. Do not assume that morality is related to activities designed to achieve cleanliness of body and mind—it is not. A moral person has a heart for God (good), and therefore his or her mind is not focused on impure thoughts. Purification of heart and mind is the basis of a person's moral character (makeup), not their personal rituals or abstinence while in the W.O.R.L.D.

Trust that I will help you to overcome any missteps in cooperation that lead to feelings of disconnection, pain, sorrow, or mental anguish. Trust that I A.M. A.B.L.E. But come to The Father in prayer humbly and with a contrite heart when these instances occur—for His L.O.V.E. is not to be taken lightly. The Power of His L.O.V.E. is not to be tested. The Power of His P.R.E.S.E.N.C.E. in you **is to be revered**. If you are aware of your limitations and exceed them, I will work within you to regain harmony and balance in L.O.V.E. through the energetic restoration of cooperation in L.O.V.E. I will wipe away all stains of transgression (indulgences) that lead to disruption of His Divine Power in you. But, be **thankful** for this, and mindful of His M.E.R.C.Y. and G.R.A.C.E. and that it is continually offered to those in My care. I A.M. your shepherd, and I A.M. responsible for bringing each of you to safety and guiding each of you H.O.M.E. (to H.I.M.). But, do not test My ability or His W.I.L.L. for you by being deliberately unaware or forgetting (abandoning) your responsibility to Be L.O.V.E.

Together, we are heavenly hosts of His power and His presence. Ask for P.E.A.C.E. of body and mind to be restored, and the counter-vibrations that occur in times of distress will disappear. T.R.U.S.T. that all is well at all T.I.M.E.s and remember (re-member) to ask for My guidance **before** you engage with anything or anyone that can disrupt your state of Being L.O.V.E. It is the best way to remain in L.O.V.E. for the duration of T.I.M.E.

Chapter 31: Trusting Versus Testing

B.E.I.N.G.: Benevolent Entity Interred in Neutral G.O.O.D.

G.O.O.D.: God's Omnipresent, Omnipotent Domain

L.O.V.E.: Light Over Vibrational Energy

M.E.: Manifest Eternity

F.A.T.H.E.R.: Forever Abiding in the Truth of Heaven's Eternal Resonance/Residence

G.R.A.C.E.: God's Resonating Alliance in C.H.R.I.S.T Eternal

C.H.R.I.S.T.: Consecrated, Holy, Resonating and Indwelling Spirit of Truth

M.E.R.C.Y.: Making Eternity Resonate Continually in You

H.I.M.: Holy Immanuel Manifested

T.R.U.S.T.I.N.G.: Truth Resonating in the Unity of the S.O.N. in T.I.M.E. and Interred in Neutral G.O.O.D.

S.O.N.: Spirit Offered in Neutrality

T.I.M.E.: Temporal Insights Meted in Eternity

M.I.N.D.: Manifest Intention from Neutral Dominion

K.I.N.G.D.O.M.: Kinetic Integration into Neutral G.O.O.D./God's Design of Omnipotent Manifestation

W.I.L.L.: Word and Intention in L.I.F.E. and L.O.V.E

L.I.F.E.: Light Inside the Fabric of Eternity

W.O.R.L.D.: War Of Rebellion in L.O.V.E.'s Domain

P.R.E.S.E.N.C.E.: Protected/Perfected Resonance Entering Sanctified Entities and Neutral, Consecrated Environments

M.Y.: Manifest Yahweh

H.O.L.Y.: Heaven's Omnipotent Light in Yahweh/You

I A.M.: Infinite Almighty Manifestation

A.B.L.E.: Abiding in the Benevolent Light of Eternity

H.O.N.O.R.: Heaven's Omnipotent Neutrality Omnipresent and Resonating

F.A.I.T.H.: Forever Accepting the Interred Truth in Him

S.U.R.R.E.N.D.E.R.: Salvation Under a Relationship Resonating Eternally in the Neutral Domain of Everlasting Reciprocity

H.O.M.E.: Holy O.N.E.s Manifesting in Emeth/Eternity

O.N.E.: Omnipresent, Neutral, Eternal

P.E.A.C.E.: Predominating Energy with Acceptance of C.H.R.I.S.T. Eternally

T.R.U.S.T.: Truth Resonating in U.N.I.T.Y. with the S.O.N. in T.I.M.E

U.N.I.T.Y.: Undying Neutral and Infinite Truth in Yahweh/You

CHAPTER 32

Trust Versus Justice

Christ says...

The Father wishes for all to come to the T.H.R.O.N.E. It is His P.R.E.S.E.N.C.E. that W.I.L.L.s it in those He has C.H.O.S.E.N. If you are B.E.I.N.G. L.O.V.E., His W.I.L.L. is for your life to be filled to the fullest extent possible with blessings from H.I.M. It is not a requirement, nor is it necessary to humble yourself before Me to be invited to abide in H.I.M., for I am not a gatekeeper in the sense that I judge or limit access. That alone is The F.A.T.H.E.R.'s right. But because I A.M. the W.A.Y. to the T.H.R.O.N.E. for all, before you can approach Him, you must T.R.U.S.T. in M.E. Trust that I A.M. A.B.L.E. Trust that all is well.

All things work together for the G.O.O.D. (God-like) in L.O.V.E. His W.I.L.L. for your life is revealed in stages as you become L.O.V.E. with M.E., and then later as you are B.E.I.N.G. L.O.V.E. with A.L.L. Once you have accepted His W.I.L.L., I A.M. A.B.L.E. to bring His blessings, those intended for you, directly to your B.E.I.N.G.

For I A.M. the W.A.Y., the Truth and the L.I.F.E. that comes from The F.A.T.H.E.R.'s right hand. I sit nearest to H.I.M., above all else, for this purpose, as well as to be the path to His T.H.R.O.N.E. My **R.E.W.A.R.D.** is to give L.I.F.E. to those in L.O.V.E. from The Giver.

R.E.W.A.R.D.: Re-membering Everything While Abiding in Resurrected Dominion

All that comes through H.I.M. to you is sent by way of The S.O.N.: I A.M. the H.A.N.D. that reaches down from the Giver of all L.I.F.E. Trust in M.E. and live abundantly. Accept His W.I.L.L. for your life and reap My R.E.W.A.R.D.

So it is that by design, I A.M. a two-way street. Become L.O.V.E. through The S.O.N. and receive L.O.V.E. through The S.O.N. This is the only means available for mankind to receive His blessings until the final day of His judgment. At that appointed time, He will declare those in L.O.V.E. to be free from all strife, and all will come to the T.H.R.O.N.E. to testify and to witness His supreme justice. I do not wish to alarm those who are reading this and are less familiar with the age-old concept of justice that the Bible describes. So, remember that justice is only a word used by man to reclaim his own sense of righteousness and balance. The F.A.T.H.E.R. needs no means of regaining balance—for all is well with H.I.M. Only man is out of balance, and therefore sees justice as a scale used to measure out punishments in retribution. The F.A.T.H.E.R. does not W.I.L.L. retribution, only L.O.V.E. So, the justice I speak of is a reference to The W.A.Y. (means) of bringing all who will respond to M.Y. invitation H.O.M.E. Justice is the restoration of mankind through whatever means necessary to reclaim you from darkness. Those who will testify will proclaim My way to be the only W.A.Y. that could ever remove the pain and suffering that man has been in; and, it is the only way to change mankind into the L.I.G.H.T. filled and L.O.V.I.N.G. B.E.I.N.G. he was intended to be. "Justice for all"[1] is a declaration of independence in America, but in The F.A.T.H.E.R.'s K.I.N.G.D.O.M., it is a declaration of U.N.I.T.Y. by all who have been C.H.O.S.E.N. in L.O.V.E. In the E.N.D., His justice for mankind (means of transformation) will be confirmed by all who have transcended and overcome the world.

Trust that you are on the path to transcendence if you abide in M.E. and I A.M. abiding in you and together we are B.E.I.N.G. L.O.V.E. The F.A.T.H.E.R.'s W.I.L.L. takes care of the rest. When He summons you to His T.H.R.O.N.E., it will be a glorious event of great magnitude, for your life's course will be changed by His declaration of L.O.V.E. and My deliverance of His **B.L.E.S.S.I.N.G.s.**

B.L.E.S.S.I.N.G.: Bountiful L.I.F.E. Entering the Sanctified and Sacred Interred in Neutral G.O.O.D.

Trust in M.E. and be A.B.L.E. to receive what He has intended for your life. But first, let me be clear about the difference between the B.L.E.S.S.I.N.G.s you assume you are receiving already.

Yes, you are blessed in many ways. But the blessings you know (experience now) are small compared to the B.L.E.S.S.I.N.G.s He wishes to bestow. Allowing M.E. into your heart and mind creates the landscape for G.R.A.C.E. and acceptance in your own B.E.I.N.G. to receive the gift of

---

[1] This is a reference to the United States of America's Pledge of Allegiance, specifically from the line "one nation under God, indivisible, with liberty and justice for all".

salvation and the blessings that come with acceptance. But the B.L.E.S.S.I.N.G.s I am referring to come from The F.A.T.H.E.R.'s declaration for your life, and they come from another level of acceptance—one born of experience in L.O.V.E. Being L.O.V.E. opens additional doors for The Giver to give. And He uses them in accordance with His W.I.L.L. for you. It has nothing to do with what you have received in life up to this point in time—for His declarations for your life come from beyond time, and as such, they are given in a different and renewed context to a renewed B.E.I.N.G. They come to you freely and without struggle or strife. They come because He has declared them to be, not because you need them to be. They come in peace and from P.E.A.C.E. They are above all things known by man, and therefore new to the experience of B.E.I.N.G. L.O.V.E., decreed by The Lover.

If you will follow M.E., I will lead you to The T.H.R.O.N.E., where S.T.R.E.A.M.s of L.I.F.E. originate and from which all B.L.E.S.S.I.N.G.s flow. You cannot approach His state of B.E.I.N.G. without M.Y. guidance and until you are being L.O.V.E. for A.L.L. Being L.O.V.E. for A.L.L. requires that you give from your own heart for the benefit of others. Giving to and for others in L.O.V.E. is the required state of B.E.I.N.G. for abiding with H.I.M. It is not a requirement for abiding with M.E., for I A.M. here to S.A.V.E., and to wipe away each stain. But until and unless you are A.B.L.E. to be L.O.V.E. at all T.I.M.E.s, you cannot approach His T.H.R.O.N.E., nor can you abide with The F.A.T.H.E.R. in the highest realms. On the final day, all who come will be L.O.V.E., for A.L.L. I.S. O.N.E., and A.L.L. I.S. L.O.V.E. and God is L.O.V.E. and I A.M. A.B.L.E. to transform, if you T.R.U.S.T. and obey L.O.V.E.

Chapter 32: Trust Versus Justice

T.H.R.O.N.E.: Trinity's H.O.L.Y., Resonance at Origin/O.N.E. (Omnipotent Neutral Energy)

H.O.L.Y.: Heaven's Omnipotent Light in Yahweh/You

O.N.E.: Omnipresent, Neutral, Eternal

P.R.E.S.E.N.C.E.: Protected/Perfected Resonance Entering Sanctified Entities and Neutral, Consecrated Environments

W.I.L.L.: Word and Intention in L.I.F.E. and L.O.V.E

L.I.F.E.: Light Inside the Fabric of Eternity

L.O.V.E.: Light Over Vibrational Energy

C.H.O.S.E.N.: Consecrated Holy Ones Seeking Eternal Neutrality

B.E.I.N.G.: Benevolent Entity Interred in Neutral G.O.O.D.

G.O.O.D.: God's Omnipresent, Omnipotent Domain

H.I.M.: Holy Immanuel Manifested

F.A.T.H.E.R.: Forever Abiding in the Truth of Heaven's Eternal Resonance/Residence

I A.M.: Infinite Almighty Manifestation

W.A.Y.: Wavelength Abiding in Yahweh/You

T.R.U.S.T.: Truth Resonating in U.N.I.T.Y. with the S.O.N. in T.I.M.E

U.N.I.T.Y.: Undying Neutral and Infinite Truth in Yahweh/You

S.O.N.: Spirit Offered in Neutrality

T.I.M.E.: Temporal Insights Meted in Eternity

M.E.: Manifest Eternity

A.B.L.E.: Abiding in the Benevolent Light of Eternity

A.L.L.: Alpha's L.O.V.E. Light

R.E.W.A.R.D.: Re-membering Everything While Abiding in Resurrected Dominion

H.A.N.D.: Heaven's Alliance in Neutral Dominion

M.Y.: Manifest Yahweh

H.O.M.E.: Holy O.N.E.s Manifesting in Emeth/Eternity

L.I.G.H.T.: L.O.V.E.'s Infinite Guardian of His Truth

L.O.V.I.N.G.: Light Overcoming Vibrations Invading/Inverting Neutral G.O.O.D.

K.I.N.G.D.O.M.: Kinetic Integration into Neutral G.O.O.D./God's Design of Omnipotent Manifestation

P.E.A.C.E.: Predominating Energy with Acceptance of C.H.R.I.S.T. Eternally

C.H.R.I.S.T.: Consecrated, Holy, Resonating and Indwelling Spirit of Truth

G.R.A.C.E.: God's Resonating Alliance in C.H.R.I.S.T Eternal

B.L.E.S.S.I.N.G.: Bountiful L.I.F.E. Entering the Sanctified and Sacred Interred in Neutral G.O.O.D.

E.N.D.: Eternal Neutral Domain

S.T.R.E.A.M.: Sanctified in Truth and Resonating Eternity's Alliance with Manifestation

S.A.V.E.: Sanctify Against Vibrational Energies

A.L.L. I.S. O.N.E.: Alpha's Love Light of Immanent Space/Spirit is Omnipotent, Neutral and Eternal

Truth

Christ says...

The way forward begins with trusting that I A.M. A.B.L.E. to deliver you from darkness. If you have tried everything else in the world, and your heart still longs for peace, then turn to M.E. and receive the gift of G.R.A.C.E. If you do not trust that I A.M. A.B.L.E., you will find that your own will asserts its own imagination of what you must do for yourself, and how you must proceed in L.O.V.E. The path designed by your own mind is fraught with pitfalls and does not lead to G.L.O.R.Y. for A.L.L. Your mind twists and turns upon itself, asking questions like... are you certain this is the way? What proof do you have that He is A.B.L.E.? What must you do, achieve, accomplish, know to be successful in L.O.V.E.? All lead to a type of striving that does not allow you to simply be L.O.V.E. Your mind tells you that you must work harder to understand before you can be for L.O.V.E. It says, "What must I know (think) about this before I can accept it and what must I understand from my own experience before I will trust it?" T.R.U.S.T. comes without understanding what is and what is next. I A.M. A.B.L.E. to take you to places that you have not yet experienced in life and do not understand from a worldly point of view because I A.M. A.B.L.E. to see A.L.L. in motion, and all that The F.A.T.H.E.R. moves for His purposes. *You are not in a position to perceive what is occurring throughout the creation. There is no other way to move beyond the condition you are in now, except to T.R.U.S.T. and to* **O.B.E.Y.** *His W.O.R.D.*

O.B.E.Y.: Overcome with Benevolent Energy in Y.O.U.

Ground yourself in His Holy word (yes, I mean the Bible), and confirmation of what I am instructing for your life will become clear. Your own instinct to live a life filled with L.I.G.H.T. and L.O.V.E. is good but limited in its ability to be L.O.V.E. at all times. I A.M. not limited. The F.A.T.H.E.R. is not limited. The creation responds to His leading, and I to His W.I.L.L. and you to M.Y. instruction for the transformation of your will into a B.E.I.N.G. that serves the creation and A.L.L. in it, rather than your own desires. Trust is at the root of the connection between us. I A.M. the vine. You are the branch.[1] *Trust that I have grafted you into the family of L.O.V.E. in a way that is strong enough to overcome all that attempts to separate us. Do not deny Me or willfully turn away from that which you understand to be the sure path, for Truth is tested by means of false doctrine. False leading takes you to a place of abstinence, a place that is not fruitful or Truth-filled and your experience of such a place will feel hollow—as though a key has been lost. Despite your searching, if you are seeking a false path, you will only find more emptiness. The only W.A.Y. to ensure your own ascension is through M.Y.*

---

[1] This is also the description Jesus gave to His disciples when comforting them about His impending departure. For reference, read the Holy Bible, John 15:5.

guiding H.A.N.D., and the only means to verify that I A.M. guiding you is to meet Me in P.R.A.Y.E.R. daily and turn to His Holy word for confirmation of what you are being led to do. If you believe that you have been guided to a place where your acceptance depends upon anything in addition to M.E., then you are believing in false doctrine-- for I A.M. the only W.A.Y. to the light of His L.O.V.E. and the B.L.E.S.S.I.N.G.S. that come through His abiding T.R.U.T.H.

T.R.U.T.H.: Trusting the Resonance that Unites T.I.M.E. with Heaven

Chapter 33: Truth

I A.M.: Infinite Almighty Manifestation
A.B.L.E.: Abiding in the Benevolent Light of Eternity
M.E.: Manifest Eternity
G.R.A.C.E.: God's Resonating Alliance in C.H.R.I.S.T.
   Eternal
C.H.R.I.S.T.: Consecrated, Holy, Resonating and
   Indwelling Spirit of Truth
L.O.V.E.: Light Over Vibrational Energy
G.L.O.R.Y.: God's L.O.V.E. Omnipresent and Resonating
   in You
A.L.L.: Alpha's L.O.V.E. Light
T.R.U.S.T.: Truth Resonating in U.N.I.T.Y. with the
   S.O.N. in T.I.M.E
U.N.I.T.Y.: Undying Neutral and Infinite Truth in
   Yahweh/You
S.O.N.: Spirit Offered in Neutrality
T.I.M.E.: Temporal Insights Meted in Eternity
F.A.T.H.E.R.: Forever Abiding in the Truth of Heaven's
   Eternal Resonance/Residence
O.B.E.Y.: Overcome with Benevolent Energy in Y.O.U.
Y.O.U.: Yahweh's Omnipresent U.N.I.T.Y.
W.O.R.D.: Wavelengths of Omnipotent Resonance and
   Dominion
L.I.G.H.T.: L.O.V.E.'s Infinite Guardian of His Truth

W.I.L.L.: Word and Intention in L.I.F.E. and L.O.V.E

L.I.F.E.: Light Inside the Fabric of Eternity

M.Y.: Manifest Yahweh

B.E.I.N.G.: Benevolent Entity Interred in Neutral G.O.O.D.

G.O.O.D.: God's Omnipresent, Omnipotent Domain

W.A.Y.: Wavelength Abiding in Yahweh/You

H.A.N.D.: Heaven's Alliance in Neutral Dominion

P.R.A.Y.E.R.: Protected/Personal Resonance Aligned with Yahweh's Eternal Resonance

B.L.E.S.S.I.N.G.: Bountiful L.I.F.E. Entering the Sanctified and Sacred Interred in Neutral G.O.O.D.

T.R.U.T.H.: Trusting the Resonance that Unites T.I.M.E. with Heaven

T.I.M.E.: Temporal Insights Meted in Eternity

Love in the Afterlife

The Father Speaks...

*When a person becomes L.O.V.E. they are walking in an eternal state of being that is powered by My energetic influence on their L.I.F.E. When they become fully immersed in M.E. there is no separation and the bonds of L.O.V.E. are so strong that they experience My unconditional acceptance, My H.E.A.R.T. and My M.I.N.D. in ways that guide their every move, every experience. This is as close as a person ever gets to unconditional "love" while in the W.O.R.L.D. But in the afterlife, A.L.L. is **W.E.L.L.***

W.E.L.L.: Walking Eternally in the Light of L.O.V.E.

---

*Nothing is lacking beyond the veil. In the heavenly realms where L.O.V.E. is A.L.L. that matters, there is a U.N.I.T.Y. that goes beyond the bond between My L.O.V.E. and the feeling of total acceptance and peace. Although that is available now, it is so much stronger in the afterlife because there is no separation between creator and created—there is O.N.L.Y. L.O.V.E. in all things. So, it is hard to imagine without being in this realm the impact on your very S.O.U.L.'s **J.O.Y.***

J.O.Y.: Jehovah's Omnipresence in You

For in M.Y. realm, your J.O.Y. is complete. As My S.O.N. said—"so that My J.O.Y. may be in you, and your J.O.Y. may be complete."[1] What is meant by this phrase is simple: stay in M.E. and I in Y.O.U. and together we will become O.N.E. So, becoming L.O.V.E. eventually leads to becoming O.N.E. And oneness is wholeness (holiness) for those who remain in the bonds of L.O.V.E. for all eternity. There is nothing to "do" but "be" in Heaven. There is nothing to fix because nothing is broken. There is life and light in everything, because L.I.F.E. and L.I.G.H.T. are everything. Science has already proven that all matter comes from energy made manifest by L.I.G.H.T.[2] [3] so there is nothing to overshadow Y.O.U. because there are no shadows. Here, there is only L.O.V.E.

*I A.M. waiting to welcome you to the house that L.O.V.E. built. Will you come to the H.O.M.E.-2 that is made of L.I.G.H.T. and live in the P.E.A.C.E. that dwells in My H.E.A.R.T. forever and ever? I hope so. I give H.O.P.E. so that Y.O.U. can simply "be" in M.E., as O.N.E. without F.E.A.R., without D.O.U.B.T. without **L.E.S.S.***

---

[1] The Father is referring to scripture here, specifically John 15:11

[2] Here the Father is referring to recent developments in science. If you are not aware of this work, here are two articles that you might find helpful. Article, Imperial London College, "Scientists Discover How to Turn Light into Matter After 80 Year Quest", May 19, 2014. By Gail Wilson.
https://www.imperial.ac.uk/news/149087/scientists-discover-teurn-light-into-matter/

[3] Article, Symmetry Magazine, "Large Hadron Collider Creates Matter from Light" August 24, 2020 by Sarah Charley:
https://www.symmetrymagazine.org/article/lhc-creates-matter-from-light

L.E.S.S.: L.I.G.H.T. Experiencing Sorrow and Suffering

So, come to the T.H.R.O.N.E. and just let M.E. L.O.V.E. you. Please, do not forsake L.O.V.E.'s invitation. You are more than you realize, and there is more than you presently S.E.E.K. If you will just S.E.E.K. M.E.—I will reveal T.R.U.T.H. on your L.I.F.E.'s path, one step at a T.I.M.E. as O.N.E. L.O.V.E. each step of the W.A.Y.

Come to the Father and say, "Yes L.O.R.D. Remake me, in M.E."

I H.O.P.E. to S.E.E. Y.O.U. S.O.O.N.

Infinity's Heavenly and Omnipresent Peaceful Energy Seeks to Experience and Enlighten (You) in Yahweh's Omnipotent Unity by the Spirit of Omnipotent, Omnipresent Neutrality

This is not the end...

If you want more, we invite you to dive deeper into God's L.O.V.E. language by joining the Becoming L.O.V.E. community on Facebook or Instagram. If you are interested in helping us extend God's L.O.V.E. to others, you may purchase a hard copy, or other L.O.V.E. inspired merchandise on our website at **www.thekeystolove.org**

Conclusion

L.O.V.E.: Light Over Vibrational Energy
L.I.F.E.: Light Inside the Fabric of Eternity
M.E.: Manifest Eternity
H.E.A.R.T.: Heaven's Eternal Alliance Resonating Truth
M.I.N.D.: Manifest Intention from Neutral Dominion
W.O.R.L.D.: War Of Rebellion in L.O.V.E.'s Domain
A.L.L.: Alpha's L.O.V.E. Light
W.E.L.L.: Walking Eternally in the Light of L.O.V.E.
U.N.I.T.Y.: Undying Neutral and Infinite Truth in
     Yahweh/You
O.N.L.Y.: Omnipresent Neutral Light in Yahweh/You
S.O.U.L.S.: Spirits Outside of U.N.I.T.Y.'s Light Source
J.O.Y.: Jehovah's Omnipresence in You
Y.O.U.: Yahweh's Omnipresent U.N.I.T.Y.
O.N.E.: Omnipresent, Neutral, Eternal
L.I.G.H.T.: L.O.V.E.'s Infinite Guardian of His Truth
H.O.M.E.-2: Holy O.N.E.s Meeting in Eternity
P.E.A.C.E.: Predominating Energy with Acceptance of
     C.H.R.I.S.T. Eternally
C.H.R.I.S.T.: Consecrated, Holy, Resonating and
     Indwelling Spirit of Truth
H.O.P.E.: Heaven's Omnipotent Perfected Energy
F.E.A.R.: Foreign Energy Altering Reality

D.O.U.B.T.: D.E.N.I.A.L. Obscuring Unrestricted
   B.E.I.N.G.s in Truth

D.E.N.I.A.L.: Damaging Energies/Entities Negating
   Infinity's Alliance with L.O.V.E.

B.E.I.N.G.: Benevolent Entity Interred in Neutral G.O.O.D.

G.O.O.D.: God's Omnipresent, Omnipotent, Domain

L.E.S.S.: L.I.G.H.T. Experiencing Sorrow and Suffering

T.H.R.O.N.E.: Trinity's H.O.L.Y., Resonance at
   Origin/O.N.E. (Omnipotent Neutral Energy)

H.O.L.Y.: Heaven's Omnipotent Light in Yahweh/You

M.E.: Manifest Eternity

S.E.E.K.: See, Experience, Enlighten, K.N.O.W.

K.N.O.W.: Know No O.T.H.E.R. Way/Wavelength

O.T.H.E.R.: Omnipresent Transmissions Heating/Hating
   Emmanuel's Resonance

T.R.U.T.H.: Trusting the Resonance that Unites T.I.M.E.
   with Heaven

T.I.M.E.: Temporal Insights Meted in Eternity

W.A.Y.: Wavelength Abiding in Yahweh/You

L.O.R.D.: L.O.V.E. Overtaking Rebellious Domains

S.E.E.: Seek, Experience, Enlighten

S.O.O.N.: Spirit of Omnipotent, Omnipresent Neutrality

Acknowledgments

I want to thank several people who have "hung in there" with me over the past dozen years as this process has unfolded. First and foremost, thanks to my friend, The Holy Spirit, who is always encouraging, never harsh and infinitely patient with me. Also, to my sister Lisa Sepulveda, who never doubted that what was happening was both real and important. Without her support and belief in me and in God and in this process, this information might never have come to fruition. Thanks to my husband Jeff who has given me the support, the room and the respect needed to freely pursue this project without judgement. Thanks to Pastor Rob Harrell who, upon hearing about this project, immediately encouraged me to continue listening and was kind enough to let me know that I was not alone and not the only person receiving a new perspective about "truth". You gave me the confidence to lean in even more, without reservation and to whole-heartedly embrace the process. Thanks to my good friend Samantha Hinrichs, an incredibly talented Creative Director who stepped up and asked how she could help bring this work to life the moment she heard about it. Much appreciation to my assistant, Deven Stiedle, who tirelessly transcribed texts from my personal journals into electronic copies for publication; and, for her intense belief in both me and the content herein. Special thanks to my life-long friend,

Meg Nollen, who traveled some of the most mysterious, intense and treacherous parts of this path with me, and yet, never wavered in her belief, fearlessness, determination, dedication and support. You are a rock Meg, and always have been. Thanks to my talented creative team who jumped in to help bring this project across the finish line, especially Bronte Giardina, Stephan Tyne, Melissa Hilgendorf and Brian Thompson. You are all very special people with much talent, love and heart to give to the world at a time when we really need it. And last but not least, thank you to my editor, Tia Smith, who immediately recognized The Word behind these words and challenged me to add footnotes and context where additional insight or reference was needed. You not only helped me see further into what was there, you also helped me connect the dots from beginning to end.

About the Author

C.H. Montgomery is the "author" of this text in the natural world and I A.M. (Infinite Almighty Manifestation) is the source of the information. She is a S.C.R.I.B.E. (Sanctified and Consecrated Receiver of Information Begat in Eternity) who brought the words contained herein to L.I.F.E. (Light Inside the Fabric of Eternity) by way of personal instruction and revelation of divine origin. She is married, lives in Austin, Texas and enjoys travel, gardening, dancing, art, interior design and cooking for family and friends. Her life-long pursuits include finding meaningful friendships, her place in the world, and how to live life with a heart that simply gives.

Made in the USA
Middletown, DE
14 April 2022